HERMAN MILLER
THE PURPOSE OF DESIGN

HERMAN MILLER
THE PURPOSE OF DESIGN

JOHN R. BERRY

RIZZOLI

First published in the United States of America in 2004
by Rizzoli International Publications, Inc.
300 Park Avenue South
New York, NY 10010
www.rizzoliusa.com

2005 2006 2007 / 10 9 8 7 6 5 4 3 2

Printed in China

ISBN: 0-8478-2654-6

Library of Congress Catalog Control Number: 2004095614

Dedicated to the hope that designers and businesses will continue to learn and prosper from each other.

And for two designers in my life:

Claudia Berry and Ray Eames at the 1984 Herman Miller picnic.

George Nelson—industrial designer, architect, author, director of design for Herman Miller. Leaving for a month's visit to Germany at the invitation of the German Government.

Charles Eames—designer, architect, film maker. Invited to visit Japan by the Japanese Government. Currently off to Germany under the auspices of the German Foreign Office.

Alexander Girard—architect, interior designer, creator of Herman Miller's fabric collection. Leaving for India to collect material for a new show at New York's Museum of Modern Art.

The extraordinary number and variety of distinctions heaped on Herman Miller's team of designers is probably unique in U.S. industry. We at Herman Miller would like to think that these are due, in part at least, to their remarkable performance in connection with the company's continuing program of research and design in furniture and fabrics.

herman **Miller,** *zeeland, mich.*

CONTENTS

FOREWORD

AS GILBERT ROHDE, HERMAN MILLER'S FIRST HEAD OF DESIGN, DECLARED, THE MOST IMPORTANT THING IN THE ROOM IS NOT THE FURNITURE—IT'S THE PEOPLE.

Matthew Pearl's inventive novel, *The Dante Club*, portrays a fictional version of Dr. Oliver Wendell Holmes pondering innocence, suffering, and sin. Holmes's deep knowledge of the human body, acquired during a long medical career, provides the lens through which he attempts to understand the human spirit. He concluded that insight into the body does not yield wisdom about the spirit. "As a doctor, Holmes never stopped appreciating how roundly defective was the design of humankind." Although achingly evident every day, the imperfect design of humankind is simply not the place to begin. Holmes was looking through the wrong end of the telescope. Humankind is too big. Broken down into its constituent parts, humankind first consists of tribes, then nations, then geographic entities like regions, states, cities, and neighborhoods—and finally, people. The problem of the design of humankind must begin with people, one by one. People alone, people in groups, people in families, and people working and playing, living together, sharing, fighting, relating, ordering and arranging and making and being. Design facilitates human relationship and relationship is how people engage and interact. People successfully engaging and interacting *is* the right end of the telescope through which to view the design of humankind.

As chronicled by John Berry, the remarkable company Herman Miller is replete with examples of the facilitation of human engagement and relationship, always beginning with people—one by one and then in groups. As Gilbert Rohde, Herman Miller's first head of design, declared, the most important thing in the room is not the furniture—it's the people.

I write these notes in my office seated at a dining table that belonged to D. J. De Pree, founder of Herman Miller. This beautiful and functional dining set, the work of Charles and Ray Eames, is part of The Herman Miller Collection, a comprehensive and wonderful design history of the company's products now housed at The Henry Ford, the museum I have the privilege to lead. The varied and rich historical holdings of The Henry Ford, including The Herman Miller Collection, comprise one of the world's great repositories of Western design tradition, with artifacts dating from earliest settlement to the end of the twentieth century. The furniture, decorative and utilitarian objects and tools, steam engines and production machines,

clothing and lighting devices, automobiles and airplanes and locomotives, and houses and workshops on exhibition at the Henry Ford Museum and in Greenfield Village all embody intention and problem-solving. The most enduring designs, whether from a "folk" tradition of shared aesthetic appropriateness or from the studios of industrial designers, all share a common attribute: they imaginatively blend the embedded careful purpose of the creator and the intended intimate "fit" for the user. This feature is found in a range of disparate objects: a hand-crafted axe handle; a one-horse, hand-painted "pleasure wagon"; an eighteenth-century Connecticut Valley chest; a Gothic-inspired steam engine; a 1936 Lincoln Zephyr automobile; and a Bill Stumpf–designed Aeron chair, another Herman Miller object that graces my office. A traditional Windsor chair in our collections, so strong yet so delicate, captures this artful combination of creator intention and user fit with its multiple vertical, pencil-thin back supports, each finely fitting into the elegantly arching back rail, each tapered at the ends. The same is true of a nineteenth-century milling machine, with Duncan Phyfe–style fluted legs cast into the iron frame and with graceful, curvilinear forms wherever the human hand of the operator met the powerful machine. Intention and fit, one by one. The same also is true of a stunningly original wheel-motif quilt by Indiana farmwoman Susan McCord, crafted at the close of the nineteenth century, anticipating the bold artistic vision of painter Paul Klee. Purposeful, careful intention; elegant, natural human fit. The Herman Miller Collection provides a marvelous coda to three centuries of three-dimensional human design presented at The Henry Ford.

Besides the focus on the needs of the individual or collective user, the Herman Miller design tradition described in John Berry's book has, for me, one other novel feature. It's not "heroic" design. It is collaborative design that is nurtured at Herman Miller. Charles Eames, one of the most celebrated design collaborators with Herman Miller, noted that design is not an individual enterprise, both because it is rooted in earlier influence and because it frequently is the result of group problem solving. Collaborative design— something we all engage in—is a shared and intimate creativity, a high-order skill. Max De Pree, who followed his father D. J. as CEO of Herman Miller, honored this trait by writing about intimacy as an essential leadership attribute in his 1989 book, *Leadership Is an Art*. "Intimacy is at the heart of competence," stated De Pree, drawing his insights on intimate leadership from the design studios and shop floors of Herman Miller.

Imaginative and intimate design teams, whose members share a traditional aesthetic or are led by a visionary design leader and who create useful and beautiful embodiments of "problems solved" for individuals and for groups, are the very essence of great design. Herman Miller's historical product catalog, like the collections of The Henry Ford, is replete with the results of this process. Two examples suffice. The famous Eames Lounge Chair is, perhaps, the quintessential vessel for solitude and reflection, endangered traits in our smalled-down, busy, networked globe. The lounge chair has provided this solitary gift for thousands and is still available, a steady seller for decades. At the opposite end of the spectrum is the Eames dining set, the perfect symbol for group engagement, whether for dialogue and debate or for breaking bread. I am happy to report that De Pree's table and chairs still regularly service these functions in my office at The Henry Ford.

A deeply learned man, Matthew Pearl's Dr. Holmes could, nevertheless, profitably revisit the problem of the design of humankind first by returning to his study of the human body and then by exploring the design cases presented here in John Berry's comprehensive book, *Herman Miller: The Purpose of Design*. For more than seventy years, Herman Miller has approached the design of humankind by focusing on the "people" through each person—one by one, then together. The right end of the telescope.

Steve Hamp
President, The Henry Ford
May 23, 2004

This image from "A Communications Primer," the 1953 film by Charles and Ray Eames, captures how each individual listens to the same input with their own set of biases and experiences. What is the purpose of design? The answer varies depending on the experience. Having a shared understanding is the first step to benefiting from the process and purpose of good design.

INTRODUCTION

DESIGN IS A PROCESS, NOT A FORMULA. IT FOLLOWS A LOGIC BUT IS OPEN TO THOSE UNEXPECTED DISCOVERIES THAT COME FROM EXPERIMENTATION AND FROM MAKING CONNECTIONS BETWEEN SEEMINGLY DISCONNECTED IDEAS.

Design is a noun, a verb, and a problem-solving process. It is art with a purpose. In order to produce solutions, design requires a clear understanding of the conditions, constraints, and opportunities of a particular situation. Good design does not happen in a vacuum. A good designer is able to recognize a need, identify the relevant limitations, and devise a solution.

The word *design* evokes a wide range of images and meanings. The term is applied to objects and processes, brands and environments, critical reviews and experiences—all of which can be good or bad. Design can be elitist or egalitarian, a profession, and a result. Any way you look at it, design in some way affects everyone.

Business, like design, is about problem-solving. The problem might be: How do I manufacture this product, share this idea, in sufficient quantity to reach consumers? How do I create and reach a market? How do I reduce my costs? How do I ensure quality? How do I organize to deliver and serve my customers? And on and on.

Herman Miller, Inc., manufactures furniture and is a truly design-driven company. It demonstrates how understanding the value of design as a problem-solving activity—rather than as mere styling—can generate new products, create new industries, develop a profession, organize a company, and redefine how we live and work. All too often, at other companies, design is relegated to the final stages of creating a product. Thoughtful design is the ingredient without which many companies fail. Too often companies do not tap the capabilities inherent in design education to help their company succeed. Common to all design professions is the desire to make something better.

At Herman Miller, design is the means *and* the end. It is the starting point and the destination. Since early in its founding, Herman Miller has embraced design as a way to improve people's lives, and through that goal, they created new industries and some of the most iconic objects of the last century. Charles and Ray Eames' Lounge Chair, George Nelson's Marshmallow Sofa, and Bill Stumpf and Don Chadwick's Aeron Chair, which populates so many offices today, are all products of Herman Miller, Inc.

Although it is not always obvious, the disciplines of design and business are symbiotic. The purpose of design is to give tangible form to ideas, and the purpose of business is to bring those tangible forms—or products—to market. Both disciplines focus on recognizing needs. When the two disciplines work together on a common need, great things are possible. Herman Miller has long known this, and many other companies that have embraced the design process have also gained a loyal customer base, financial success, and high visibility. Apple Computer, with its iMac and iPod, meets technology needs through great engineering, intuition, and good graphics. OXO Good Grips, with its highly functional kitchen tools, meets the needs of arthritic hands through large, comfortable handles and ends up serving everyone. These companies have made design a fundamental part of their product development, and have reaped rewards from that thinking.

This book presents fourteen specifically chosen case studies that embody the problem-solving ethos of Herman Miller, Inc. It is by no means a comprehensive survey of Herman Miller's output, or even a collection of all-stars. Each initiative presented here started with identifying a need—to furnish a new type of living space, for healthier seating, for a new organization—and then met it. Some of these efforts led to commercially successful products; others led to creative ideas and discoveries that influenced later projects. Best known for home and office furniture, Herman Miller has also created a profession, developed their own working environment as a living laboratory, fostered an inclusive work environment, and led the way for a fresh approach to graphic design. This democratic definition of design has provided Herman Miller with multiple successes.

Unlike fine art, which an artist produces for himself with the hope that others will appreciate it, good design must focus on mass-production or, in the case of architecture, serving a large and varied public. That is why the best design is closely entwined with business, and few companies represent that relationship more clearly or more successfully than Herman Miller. Designers and businesspeople can learn lessons from these examples.

The Evolution of Herman Miller

Herman Miller never worked at Herman Miller. He was, however, a real person. He was the father-in-law of D.J. De Pree. De Pree started working at the Star Manufacturing Company in 1909 right out of high school, to do general office work. (Star Manufacturing, with a factory in Zeeland, Michigan, and a showroom in Grand Rapids, made reproductions of European bedroom, living room, and dining room furniture. Their biggest client was Sears.) In 1914 De Pree married Nellie Miller. He worked his way up to become the company's president five years later. In 1923, at De Pree's urging, Herman Miller, a businessman, put together a group that bought the shares of Star's majority stockholder. They then convinced other shareholders to sell their shares to them as well. De Pree, new owner and president, renamed the company Herman Miller, Inc., after the reputable man who had made the transaction possible.

Star Manufacturing was one of several furniture companies in West Michigan. Dutch immigrants had settled the area and were largely cabinet-makers well skilled in woodworking. The furniture produced was either copied from or inspired by Victorian and eighteenth-century furniture found in the large homes of wealthy European families. The pieces were grand in scale and ornate in decoration with carvings, inlays, veneers, moldings, and hand finishes.

For the first few years, Herman Miller continued to produce the same furniture that Star had. However, the Depression quickly brought the company close to bankruptcy. In 1931, Gilbert Rohde, a commercial artist from New York who had turned to designing furniture, presented himself to De Pree, showed his "modern" furniture designs, and convinced De Pree that the trends of the future were clean, simple lines—furniture that was easy to move and could accommodate changing lifestyles. De Pree believed in Rohde's vision, and the two men began a collaboration that created what we think of today as mid-century modern furniture.

Rohde and other industrial designers in the 1930s were strongly influenced by European modernism. For years, most notably at the Bauhaus, Europeans had pursued a new aesthetic for the modern age. They believed that the new materials, new manufacturing processes, and new construction techniques grown out of the Industrial Revolution demanded a new formal language. Machine-made furniture from a factory in the twentieth century should not resemble the hand-carved wood pieces that had been made in the eighteenth, and those that did were false or dishonest. Victorian and early American furniture styles had no place in the new industrialized era. Beauty, designers preached, lay in revealing, not covering up, the way something was made.

De Pree's openness to this new design thinking set the course for Herman Miller's future, and it demonstrated how a company can not only grow but also thrive in collaboration with designers.

Working with Designers

Although a thoroughly design-centric company, Herman Miller does not employ its product designers as staff. Even George Nelson, titled Design Director for many years, worked from his New York office and was involved with other companies. Instead, designers work with Herman Miller's employees, specialized experts in related fields—engineering, materials science, ergonomics, psychology, manufacturing, marketing and so on. Outside designers are contracted for specific projects focused on specific issues. The ability to recognize needs can be easier from outside a company. Concerns for pleasing an employer might outweigh solving a business problem. It is the shared respect between designer and company managers that allows for the best results.

Perhaps no designers embody Herman Miller's problem-solving approach more than Charles and Ray Eames. In 1972, Herman Miller worked with the Eameses to produce a five-minute film called *Design Q&A*. It was based on Charles Eames's answers to questions posed by curators of the Louvre's 1967 exhibition *What Is Design?*, which aimed to explain the design process to museum visitors. Although the film's visuals are provocative, it is the text that lays out the case for design being about problem-solving and offers a concise understanding of Eames's views.

Q. What is your definition of design, Monsieur Eames?
A. One could describe design as a plan for arranging elements to accomplish a particular purpose.

Q. Is design an expression of art?
A. I would rather say it's an expression of purpose. It may, if it is good enough, be later judged as art.

Q. Is design a craft for industrial purposes?
A. No, but design may be a solution to some industrial problem.

Q. What are the boundaries of design?
A. What are the boundaries of problems?

Q. Is design a discipline that concerns itself with only one part of the environment?

A. No.

Q. Is it a method of general expression?

A. No, it is a method of action.

Q. Is design a creation of an individual?

A. No, because to be realistic one must always recognize the influence of those that have gone before.

Q. Is design a creation of a group?

A. Very often.

Q. Is there a design ethic?

A. There are always design constraints and these often imply an ethic.

Q. Does design imply the idea of products that are necessarily useful?

A. Yes, even though the use might be very subtle.

Q. Is it able to cooperate in the creation of works reserved solely for pleasure?

A. Who would say that pleasure is not useful?

Q. Ought form to derive from the analysis of function?

A. The great risk here is that the analysis may be incomplete.

Q. Can the computer substitute for the designer?

A. Probably, in some special cases, but usually the computer is an aid to the designer.

Q. Does design imply industrial manufacture?

A. Not necessarily.

Q. Is design used to modify an old object through new techniques?

A. This is one kind of design problem.

Q. Is design used to fix up an existing model so that it is more attractive?

A. One doesn't usually think of design in this way.

Q. Is design an element of industrial policy?

A. If design constraints imply an ethic, and if industrial policy includes ethical principles, then yes, design is an element of industrial policy.

Q. Does the creation of design admit constraints?

A. Design depends largely on constraints.

Q. What constraints?

A. The sum of all constraints. Here is one of the few effective keys to the design problem: the ability of the designer to recognize as many of the constraints as possible; his willingness and enthusiasm for working within these constraints—the constraints of price, of size, of strength, of balance, of surface, of time, and so forth. Each problem has its own peculiar list.

Q. Does design obey laws?

A. Aren't constraints enough?

Q. Are there tendencies and schools in design?

A. Yes, but these are more a measure of human limitations than ideals.

Q. Is design ephemeral?

A. Some needs are ephemeral. Most designs are ephemeral.

Q. Ought design to tend toward the ephemeral or toward permanence?

A. Those needs and designs that have a more universal quality tend toward relative permanence.

Q. How would you define yourself with respect to a decorator? An interior architect? A stylist?

A. I wouldn't.

Q. To whom does design address itself: to the greatest number? To the specialist or the enlightened amateur? To a privileged social class?

A. Design addresses itself to the need.

Q. After having answered all these questions, do you feel that you have been able to practice the profession of design under satisfactory, or even optimum conditions?

A. Yes.

Q. Have you been forced to accept compromises?

A. I don't remember ever being forced to accept compromises, but I have willingly accepted constraints.

Q. What do you feel is the primary condition for the practice of design and for its propagation?

A. A recognition of need?

Q. What is the future of design?

A. [In the film, no answer is provided, only a pointed silence.]

Once they had identified a problem, the Eameses were tenacious. They studied it from every angle until they landed on what they believed was the best solution. They took what time was needed, or allocated for a short time project. Charles Eames, considered the most influential designer of the twentieth century, responded to a question about his presumed quick intuitive design idea behind the now-famous Lounge Chair with, "Yes, it was a flash of genius—about a thirty-year flash."

Another designer who was central to defining Herman Miller's philosophy was George Nelson. For many years, Nelson served as the company's Head of Design. On my first day of work at Herman Miller, in 1980, the CEO, Max De Pree, son of D.J. asked Nelson to spend the rest of the week giving me an orientation to the organization. By this time, Nelson was 72 years old, a consultant and a legend. The next morning George came into my office, cane in hand, and said, "So you're Berry. . . . I'm supposed to orient you. Okay, here goes. There are too many highly paid executives and too many highly paid consultants. I'm one of them. Done with orientation." After we laughed, he became more introspect. He told me that the company was complex and always changing, as it should be; that it was focused mostly on the right things—figuring out the problems ahead—and not on what was merely possible with existing manufacturing capabilities. He suggested that the best orientation would come from direct experience. He encouraged me to work in the plant for awhile, and I did.

Before Herman Miller, my experience included design studies at Indiana University, Cranbrook Academy of Art, the investigation of the psychology of color, and thirteen years with a large architectural firm. George, who was trained as an architect, was intrigued with color and space, and as we talked, I realized that our conversation was one of those rare, pivotal times when you're exposed to the mind of someone who sees things in wonderfully new ways. George had a crisp vision of the future workplace, the implications of technology on the way people worked, and how offices were affected by different sounds, enclosures, lighting, and color. He was the first to tell me why people's eyes feel tired when they go home and sit in front of their television sets. He said that the eye, like other organs, was naturally relaxed when it was doing its job, which was to open and close to adapt to the changes in light levels among trees, leaves, and caves. Office work, done under nearly constant lighting, creates strain on the eye, and when you go home in the evening and watch television, with its rapidly changing images, your eye continually flexes back and forth, causing the eye to relax. I thought this was fascinating, as were most subjects that George discussed during that week.

In many ways, it was that week with George that led to this book. Our conversations cemented the idea in my mind that a better bridge was needed between the worlds of business and design. As part of my experiences with Herman Miller, now spanning more than twenty-three years, I've been fortunate to participate with a company that is concerned about, identifies, and resolves problems in our living, working, and built environments.

George Nelson and I both felt strongly that design education and business education needed a closer relationship. The Herman Miller company also valued education—both for their customers and for their employees. Herman Miller products were often so innovative that architects and interior designers needed to be introduced to them with an explanation of their revolutionary features. Internally, the company provided continual education to its employees. They even bought an estate on the shores of Lake Macatawa and converted it into a learning center called Marigold. A few years after joining Herman Miller, I began to conceptualize a "Short Course on Design for Non-Designers" in discussion with George Nelson, Ray Eames, design writer and historian Ralph Caplan, and others at Marigold. Although in the end, the class did not come to fruition, the intent behind it is part of this book.

Herman Miller did try an experiment in the early 1980s with George Nelson teaching a class at the University of Michigan for graduate students from the business and architecture departments to come together for a special assignment. They were to collectively solve a hypothetical problem posed by Nelson. The class failed due to the very problems it was intended to overcome: business students assumed that architects were too concerned with aesthetics, and architects assumed that business students didn't appreciate the effects or implications of physical space.

The general public often thinks about design just as styling, but styling—making something look better—is merely superficial. A design professor of mine at Indiana University, George Sadek, used a term to describe the results of bad design: "bumper design." He pointed out that if cars were designed well, they would not need bumpers, and if bumpers were designed well, they would not need bumper guards. But poor design, by contrast, required exactly such stylistic additions without meeting the original need. Charles Eames once said, "The degree to which a designer has a style is the degree to which they didn't solve the problem."

In the catalog that accompanied a 1983 exhibition called *Design Since 1945*, for which George Nelson designed the installation, George wrote, "The aim of the design process is always to produce an object that does something. In problem solving, the limitations are far more important than the freedoms. The only creative freedom that is worth anything is found in setting up a problem so that it can be solved intelligently." Good design has common characteristics: functionality, economical use of materials, efficient manufacturing processes, and visual appeal.

Design is a process, not a formula. It follows a logic but is open to those unexpected discoveries that come from experimentation and from making connections between seemingly disconnected ideas. The Eameses built numerous prototypes for any project on which they worked and used photography to study the visual appeal of shapes, material connections, and how pieces of the whole worked together.

This book covers the period from 1931, when D.J. De Pree, the founder of Herman Miller, recognized the value of a new approach to design, to 2003 and the introduction of the Mirra chair. The examples of design address seemingly simple and unrelated issues—furniture for a changing society, uses of new materials such as molded plywood, a changing work environment, needs of an aging population, comfortable, healthy long-term seating, and the establishment of a new profession to deal with the changes in the workplace. What unifies all of them is the problem-solving philosophy behind them.

Most histories of design recognize just the end products suitable for museums and appreciated by many, but often fail to present the reasons the product came to exist, the processes required to create this design, and the kind of business collaboration that brings a good idea into being. The history of Herman Miller, Inc., on the other hand, focuses more on the genesis of a product, because the product's lasting value stems from that original inspiration that met an understood need. The proof of the value comes in the marketplace, where many of Herman Miller's earlier products are still sought, some having been in continual production for almost sixty years, and new products are continually in process.

Gilbert Rohde's design leadership at Herman Miller gave the company an entirely new direction for products. It took a while for the Herman Miller sales force to learn how to sell the new style of furniture, which was relatively expensive. It caught on, though, as the country began to embrace new materials, new manufacturing techniques, a new aesthetic, and the recognition of the needs being met.

After Gilbert Rohde died unexpectedly in 1944, De Pree searched for a new Head of Design. He read an article in *Life* magazine (Jan. 22, 1945) about a concept for built-in storage walls designed by George Nelson. The article seemed to echo much of what Rohde had believed about new lifestyles demanding new space utilization. De Pree and Jimmy Eppinger, Herman Miller's salesperson, first met with Nelson to discuss the design job. Nelson said he was flattered, but he had never heard of the Herman Miller company. An architect by training, he was not terribly interested in designing furniture and had never been inside a furniture factory. Over many months, De Pree and Nelson continued to talk, and in 1944 Nelson became Director of Design for Herman Miller, living and working in New York, with the company's factory in Zeeland, Michigan. In Nelson's first year in his new role, he was prolific. He produced seventy-seven designs, a rate unmatched to this day.

Nelson also brought new ideas about the kind of company Herman Miller should become. He believed a company that was providing quality furniture should provide a quality experience in all elements that represented the company, including showrooms, catalogs, letterhead, the experiences of planning, specifying, the interactions with architects, interior designers, and the end users of the products. George provided the logic of a corporate identity program before the term *corporate identity* existed. He put together a catalog that listed product dimensions and information about each piece and featured fine photography; no catalog like it previously existed. He had it bound in a hardcover and sold it. Years later he said he knew the catalog was a success when Knoll produced a similar one about six months later.

It was Nelson, more than any other designer, who persuaded Herman Miller to take advantage of the full breadth of design talents that can be brought to bear on a business. While Gilbert Rohde certainly provided the first awareness of the value of problem solving, Nelson extended that thinking into all of the aspects of an organization. George brought in Charles and Ray Eames, Isamu Noguchi, Alexander Girard, and others to the Herman Miller team. All of these designers were free to develop concepts and ideas that they believed would improve the human condition. That was the need and collaboration was the approach.

The Example of Design

I have, over the years, interacted with or served as a consultant to major manufacturers in the furniture industry. Along with my intimate knowledge of Herman Miller, this has provided me with a basis for comparison. It is easy for me to say that Herman Miller, more than any other office furniture company that I know, trusts its designers, believes in research and the vision of its employees, and prides itself on enabling good design. The company collaborates with design thought leaders, providing engineering, technology support, and the complement of multiple disciplines that work together on the common problem at hand.

The case studies that follow present the recognized needs, and how a team of people, typically led by one or two visionary designers, address that problem and accomplish a solution. It is no accident that the products of Herman Miller have lasted for decades. When a designer is allowed to uncover the root of a given problem, his or her solution is bound to have enduring results. Herman Miller's approach is not about creating a fad or a fashion, but recognizing real, and changing needs.

This book is not meant to be a history. It is not meant to be a chronology. It is not about the many people who have influenced the company as employees and consultants. It is meant to provide a conceptual bridge between design and business and show that successful results can come from dissimilar disciplines working on a common problem. I've always believed that a designer—as a problem solver or an organization leader or a project director—has an edge over others because designers gather input, are open to so many new ideas and are schooled in the benefits of bringing different elements together. Designers should see themselves as leaders, not followers, as problem solvers, not stylists. Businesses should see designers as strategic partners, not a department, as holistic thinkers, not decorators. As part of the beginning of an activity not as the end that makes something look nice.

The integration of design and business continues to elude many corporations, as well as business schools and design schools, across the country. The successful results of the symbiotic relationship between the two disciplines are often recognized but represent too small a percentage of produced products. The examples of successful solutions in this book underscore the value of integrating business and design.

Herman Miller's history is also filled with examples of products that were seemingly in competition with other Herman Miller products. While this was often true, the company's decision to make the competing products came from the fact that they were such good products. The company was less concerned with poaching part of its own market share than with providing new and innovative solutions for what Gilbert Rohde called the most important element of a room: the people.

As a result, Herman Miller has enjoyed tremendous success and garnered lasting respect from the public, its customers, and other businesses. Only when consumer-goods companies allow design to be an influence at the highest levels of the organization will they maximize their potential as an organization.

Because of Herman Miller's corporate philosophy of collaboration, the work that follows can be enjoyed on a number of levels all at once: as aesthetic ideals, as ingenious solutions, as an optimistic view of seeing problems as opportunities, as the results of a managed process, and as financially successful products of a focused research-and-development process.

FIRST, THERE WAS...

Period Furniture

BUT THEN IT ALL CHANGED...

1905

Star Furniture Company, a manufacturer of high quality traditional-style bedroom suites, opens for business in Zeeland, Michigan.

1909

Star Furniture Company is renamed Michigan Star Furniture Company. The company hires Dirk Jan (D.J.) De Pree as a clerk. De Pree is 18 years old.

1919

**D.J. De Pree is named president of
Michigan Star Furniture Company.**

1923

Michigan Star Furniture Company becomes the Herman Miller Furniture Company when D.J. De Pree convinces his father-in-law, Herman Miller, to purchase the majority of shares of Michigan Star Furniture Company. De Pree becomes the first president of the Herman Miller Furniture Company, which continues to manufacture reproductions of traditional home furniture.

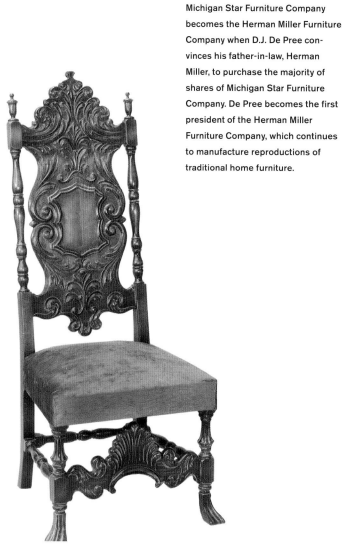

1927

A millwright dies on the job.
De Pree visits the family, where
the millwright's widow reads poetry
authored by her husband. De Pree,
deeply moved, makes a commitment
to treat all workers as individuals
with special talents and potential.
The story of the millwright becomes
part of Herman Miller lore.

D.J. De Pree founds the Herman
Miller Clock Company. The clock
company makes traditionally
designed clocks and later adds
Gilbert Rohde designs.

1930

Herman Miller, like many companies, faces failure amid the turmoil of the Great Depression. De Pree, looking for a way to save the company, receives a visit by Gilbert Rohde, a designer from New York, at Herman Miller's Grand Rapids showroom. Rohde convinces De Pree to move away from traditional furniture and to focus on products better suited to the changing needs and lifestyles of Americans.

1933

Herman Miller debuts its Rohde-
designed furniture at the Century of
Progress Exposition in Chicago.

1937

D.J. De Pree turns the Herman Miller Clock Company over to his brother-in-law, Howard Miller, who renames it the Howard Miller Clock Company.

1939

Herman Miller opens a showroom in Chicago's Merchandise Mart.

1942

The Executive Office Group,
designed by Gilbert Rohde,
signals Herman Miller's entry
into the office-furniture market.
Modular and versatile, EOG is
a precursor of systems furniture.

Charles and Ray Eames, working
in Los Angeles to produce molded
plywood furniture, are commissioned
by the Navy to develop lightweight,
molded plywood leg splints.

Herman Miller's Los Angeles
showroom opens.

1944

Gilbert Rohde dies, De Pree begins
searching for a new design leader.

1945

After seeing an article in *Life* magazine on George Nelson and his Storagewall design, D.J. De Pree hires him to serve as the company's first design director.

1946

The Nelson Office designs the stylized "M" logo and introduces a new corporate image for Herman Miller.

Nelson and De Pree recruit Charles and Ray Eames into the Herman Miller fold.

The Eames molded plywood chair, molded plywood lounge chair, molded plywood folding screen, and molded plywood coffee table are introduced.

The Nelson platform bench is introduced.

New York's Museum of Modern Art installs a small exhibition called "New Furniture Designed by Charles Eames," the museum's first one-man furniture show.

1947

Herman Miller gains exclusive market and distribution rights to the Eameses' award-winning molded plywood products. These rights are acquired from the Evans Products Company of Venice, California, which retains production rights.

1948

Herman Miller publishes and sells a bound, hardcover product catalog, written by George Nelson and designed by the Nelson Office. The catalog, which articulates Herman Miller's philosophy and principles about business and design, will become a collector's item.

Herman Miller introduces a glass-topped coffee table designed by Isamu Noguchi.

From the collection of fabrics and wallpapers designed by Alexander Girard for Herman Miller.

1949

Molded plywood manufacturing operation moves from Evans Products to Herman Miller. A plant is set up in Venice, California, which later becomes the Eames Studio.

1950

Herman Miller becomes the first company in Michigan to adopt the Scanlon Plan, a program of participative management and gain sharing. This begins a long relationship with Dr. Carl Frost, who will guide the company's participative endeavors for many years.

The world's first molded fiberglass chairs, designed by Charles and Ray Eames, are introduced by Herman Miller. Eames storage units and wire base tables are introduced.

1951

Herman Miller begins its long association with Alexander Girard, noted colorist and textile designer.

The Eames elliptical table is introduced.

1952

Girard leads the newly formed Herman Miller Textile Division.

Nelson bubble lamps are introduced.

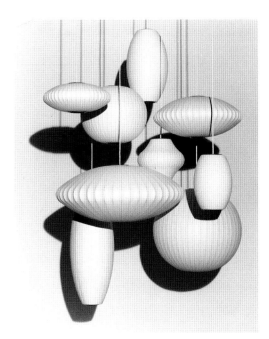

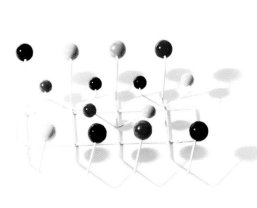

1953

Girard wallpapers and the Eames Hang-It-All are introduced.

1954

Nelson pedestal tables and the Eames sofa compact are introduced.

1955

Nelson coconut and flying duck chairs and Eames stacking/ hanging chairs are introduced.

Eames storage units are discontinued. They will be reintroduced in 1998.

The Eames molded plywood folding screen is discontinued. It will be reintroduced in 1994.

1956

The Eames lounge chair and ottoman are introduced on national television on NBC's *The Arlene Francis Home Show*. The chair is to become a highly visible emblem of Herman Miller quality and innovation.

The Nelson marshmallow sofa is introduced.

Time clocks are removed from Herman Miller's manufacturing sites.

1957

The Eames molded plywood chair, molded plywood lounge chair, and molded plywood coffee table are discontinued. They will be reintro-duced in 1994.

Herman Miller begins selling its products to the European market.

1958

Eames aluminum group chairs are introduced.

Herman Miller begins building its Zeeland headquarters complex. George Nelson is the primary architect. A new plant opens in Venice, California, and a showroom opens in San Francisco.

Robert Propst becomes a Herman Miller researcher.

1959

Nelson's Comprehensive Storage System, which uses vertical space to free up living space, is introduced.

1960

The Herman Miller Furniture Company incorporates, becoming Herman Miller, Inc. The Herman Miller Research Division, which will later become the Herman Miller Research Corporation, opens in Ann Arbor, Michigan, as a wholly owned sub-sidiary. Its president is inventor and teacher Robert Propst.

Eames walnut stools are introduced.

1961

Herman Miller's textiles and accessories retail shop, the Textiles and Objects Shop (a.k.a. T & O), opens in New York City.

The Eames Hang-It-All is discontinued. It will be reintroduced in 1994.

1962

Hugh De Pree, son of D.J., assumes leadership of Herman Miller, Inc., as president and chief executive officer. D.J. becomes chairman of the board.

Eames tandem sling seating is introduced and installed at Chicago's O'Hare Airport.

1964

Bob Propst and George Nelson work together on the first prototypes of Action Office 1, a group of freestanding units that will evolve into the Action Office system.

The Eames elliptical table is discontinued. It will be reintroduced in 1994.

The Nelson sling sofa is introduced. Eames dining tables are introduced.

1965	1966	1967	1968
The marshmallow sofa is discontinued. It will be reintroduced in 1999.	With nearly one hundred fifty dealers, Herman Miller has expanded its presence to Central and South America, Australia, Canada, Europe, Africa, the Near East, Scandinavia, and Japan.	In Switzerland, Herman Miller introduces the Panton chair, a single-form, completely plastic chair. It will be sold until 1975. The Nelson platform bench is discontinued. It will be reintroduced in 1994.	Herman Miller introduces the Action Office system, the world's first open-plan modular system of panels and attaching components. Designed by Robert Propst, AO, as it will come to be called, will revolutionize office design and spawn a whole new industry. Robert Propst's book, *The Office: A Facility Based on Change*, is published. The Eames chaise is introduced.

1969

Herman Miller, United Kingdom, forms. It has sales and marketing responsibilities throughout the United Kingdom and Scandinavia. A new showroom opens in Osaka, Japan.

Eames soft pad chairs are introduced.

D.J. De Pree steps down as chairman of the board. Hugh De Pree becomes the new chairman.

1970

Herman Miller, Inc., offers stock to the public. Charles Eames designs the stock certificate.

Herman Miller opens a new facility in Bath, England.

1971

Herman Miller enters the health/ science market with the introduction of the Co/Struc system, based on a concept originated by Bob Propst in the 1960s.

1973

Eames soft pad lounge chairs, executive tables, and segmented base rectangular tables are introduced.

The Noguchi coffee table is discontinued. It will be reintroduced in 1984.

1974

Chadwick modular seating, designed by Don Chadwick, is introduced.

Rapid Response becomes the industry's first quick-ship program.

1975

A major exhibition, "Nelson, Eames, Girard, Propst: The Design Process at Herman Miller," opens at the Walker Art Center in Minneapolis.

1976

Herman Miller introduces the Ergon chair, and a new era of ergonomic seating begins.

Star Industries, later called Integrated Metal Technology, becomes a Herman Miller subsidiary. Building C is added to the main site.

The Design of Herman Miller, by Ralph Caplan, is published by the Whitney Library of Design.

1979

Herman Miller opens the Facility Management Institute in Ann Arbor, Michigan, helping establish the profession of facility management.

Nelson bubble lamps are discontinued. They will be reintroduced in 1998.

1980

A new Holland seating plant is built. The Building B production site is converted to office space.

Max De Pree becomes chief executive officer.

1981

V-Wall movable walls are introduced.

Burdick Group is introduced.

1982

Vaughan Walls, Inc., a manufacturer of movable, modular walls, becomes a Herman Miller subsidiary.

Tradex, Inc., becomes a Herman Miller subsidiary, providing a trade-in ability of used furniture systems for new. Its name is later changed to Phoenix Designs and then to Miller SQA, providing easy-to-acquire work-stations, casegoods, and seating.

1983

Herman Miller purchases Miltech, a manufacturer of data-processing and computer-support furniture.

A special stock-ownership plan establishes all Herman Miller employees as shareholders.

1984

Herman Miller opens facilities in England and France and a distribu-tion center in Dayton, New Jersey.

Response Plus is added to the quick-ship program.

The Equa chair, the Ethospace system, and the Eames sofa are introduced.

1985

The Worldesign Congress names Charles Eames "The Most Influential Designer of the Century" and Action Office "The Most Significant Design" since 1960.

Dealerships open in Korea, Malaysia, and Australia.

Milcare, a wholly owned subsidiary, is formed from the company's Health/Science Division, which began in 1971.

1986

Herman Miller is named a Fortune 500 company.

Fortune magazine establishes furniture manufacturing as a category; Herman Miller is named Most Admired.

Construction of the Design Yard in Holland, Michigan, begins.

The Custom Choices Division is established to offer nonstandard products.

The Scooter stand and the Proper chair are introduced.

George Nelson dies.

1987

Action Office enhancements become Action Office Encore (later renamed Action Office Series 2).

Newhouse Group furniture is introduced.

1988

Ergon 2 chairs and Ethospace support cabinets are introduced.

Ray Eames dies.

Max De Pree publishes *Leadership Is an Art.*

Former senior vice president and long-term employee Dick Ruch becomes CEO.

1989

Hollington chairs are introduced.

The Equa chair wins a Design of the Decade award from *Time* magazine.

1990

Meridian becomes a Herman Miller subsidiary.

D.J. De Pree dies.

1991

Relay furniture and Action Office Series 3 products are introduced.

Sanford, formerly a Helikon Furniture manufacturing operation in Sanford, North Carolina, begins manufacturing Herman Miller wood casegoods.

1992

J. Kermit Campbell becomes Herman Miller's fifth CEO and president— the first person from outside the company to hold either post.

Herman Miller UK earns an ISO 9002 registration.

Herman Miller launches Valuing Uniqueness, a workshop on diversity in the workplace.

Great office furniture without hunting.

S Q A

1993

Herman Miller and Meridian earn ISO 9001 registrations.

Geneva casegoods, later renamed Madeira, are introduced.

Alexander Girard dies.

The company's first Environmental Conference is held.

The Liaison Cabinet System is introduced at NeoCon.

1994

Herman Miller, Inc., introduces the Aeron chair and the New York Museum of Modern Art adds it to its 20th Century Design Collection. Phoenix Designs introduces the Avian chair.

Herman Miller for the Home is formed. It markets products to the residential market, including reintroduced products from the 1940s, 50s, and 60s.

Herman Miller buys Righetti, a wholly owned subsidiary in Mexico; closes its manufacturing and warehouse facilities in Ft. Worth, Texas, and Dayton, New Jersey; and begins construction of its new Phoenix Designs building. This building, in Holland, Michigan, later becomes Miller SQA and, in 1999, the Herman Miller GreenHouse.

The company receives the National Wildlife Federation Award.

1995

Ergon 3, Equa 2, and Ambi chairs are introduced. The Beirise Collection is introduced.

Max De Pree retires from the Board of Directors. J. Kermit Campbell resigns as CEO. Mike Volkema becomes CEO.

Herman Miller's website, www.hermanmiller.com, goes live.

1996

Arrio freestanding systems furniture is introduced.

The new Miller SQA manufacturing and office building begins operations.

The Home Office program begins.

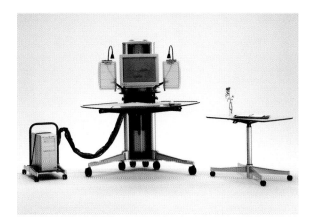

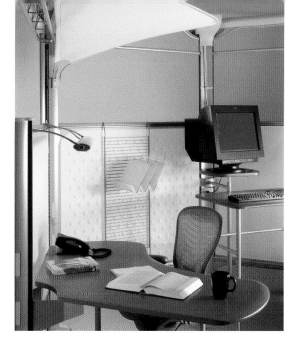

1997

Herman Miller for the Home introduces the Beirise Collection.

For the ninth time in ten years, *Fortune* magazine names Herman Miller "most admired" furniture company in the U.S.

Herman Miller and Geiger Brickel, a high-quality wood casegoods and seating manufacturer headquartered in Atlanta, Georgia, enter a strategic sales alliance.

1998

Herman Miller introduces Passage furniture, Aeron and Ambi side chairs, Accents Collection ergonomic support products, CLT tables, the TJ Collection, and the Puzzle mobile workstation, and displays the Levity Collection (then named Acrobat suite) at NeoCon.

Herman Miller for the Home introduces Meinecke rugs and increases its classics offering by adding Eames storage units, Nelson bubble lamps, and pillows, scrims, and table runners in textiles designed by Alexander Girard.

Miller SQA introduces the Reaction work chair and the Aside side chair.

Meridian, Milcare, Miller SQA, Coro, and Performis—former subsidiaries—become part of Herman Miller, Inc. The Meridian brand name is retained, Milcare becomes Herman Miller for Healthcare, and SQA becomes a brand name for Herman Miller's mid-market efforts—a market brand used by a specific set of dealers.

Herman Miller International introduces the Verve freestanding desk system in Europe.

1999

Herman Miller introduces the Kiva Collection, Caper chairs, Ergon 3 Extra-size work chair, Meridian 140 and 160 Series pedestals and displays the Resolve system at NeoCon.

Herman Miller for the Home introduces the Newhouse Home Office Collection, Newhouse Windsor chair, and Goetz sofa, and reintroduces the Nelson marshmallow sofa.

Herman Miller buys Geiger Brickel.

The Aeron chair wins a Design of the Decade award from *Business Week* magazine and the Industrial Designers Society of America (IDSA).

2000

Herman Miller RED (www.herman-millerred.com) is launched—a small business-focused branch of Herman Miller, offering quality products, quickly and inexpensively. Products are available exclusively online, with a single retail store located in New York.

Employee stock option is offered, July 2000. HMI sales reach nearly $2 billion (1.95).

The Eames molded plywood chair is named "design of the century" by *Time* magazine.

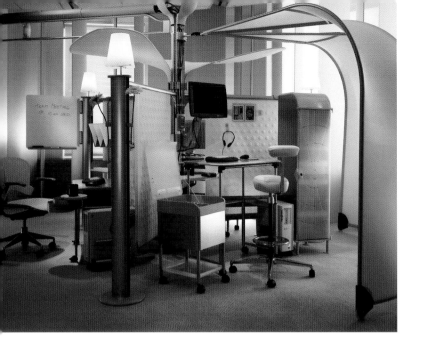

2001

DOT (Design on Textile) program, which allows customer customization of work environments, is introduced, initially with the Resolve Office System.

Herman Miller Resolve system is added to the Museum of Modern Art's permanent collection, and to the collection of the Brooklyn Museum of Art.

2002

Herman Miller is again named Fortune's Most Admired Furniture Company. This marks the fifteenth time in sixteen years that Herman Miller has earned the number one ranking on this prestigious list.

Herman Miller's C-1 corporate office facility renovation receives Gold LEED (Leadership in Energy and Environmental Design) Green Building certification, only the tenth Gold standard awarded nationwide.

Herman Miller opens the Market-Place, a leased, built-to-suit office facility near its Mainsite headquarters in Zeeland, Michigan. Designed as an open, airy, and people-focused structure that also incorporates a number of environmentally sound principles, the MarketPlace soon becomes a "must-see" destination for customers, dealers, and others visiting Herman Miller in West Michigan.

Herman Miller introduces PostureFit, a major ergonomic breakthrough in seating designed to support a healthful posture and significantly improve lower back comfort. The PostureFit technology is offered as an option on Herman Miller's Aeron chair. A passive version will become part of every Mirra chair.

2003

Herman Miller introduces Mirra, a high-performing, environmentally advanced work chair and the first piece of office furniture to be developed from its inception according to cradle-to-cradle principles.

The Mirra chair wins the Best of NeoCon Gold Award.

The Herman Miller MarketPlace receives Gold LEED Certification. At the time, it is one of less than a dozen buildings nationwide to achieve that distinction.

2004

For the sixteenth time in eighteen years, Herman Miller is ranked as the "Most Admired" company in the furniture industry in *Fortune* magazine's annual survey. The magazine also ranks Herman Miller among the most innovative companies in any industry, placing the firm fourth overall among the nearly six hundred companies surveyed.

Herman Miller receives GreenGuard Indoor Air Quality certification for most of its products.

For the fifth year in a row, Herman Miller ranks among *Business Ethics* magazine's "One Hundred Best Corporate Citizens"—one of only twenty-nine companies to earn a place on the list every year since its introduction in 2000.

The American Institute of Architects (AIA) includes Building C-1 at Herman Miller's Mainsite headquarters among its Top Ten Green Building Projects for the year. Built in 1974, C-1 completed a significant renovation in 2003.

Herman Miller introduces the "Intersect Portfolio" freestanding products that support collaboration.

Brian Walker becomes CEO.

CHAPTER 1 : A NEW SCHEME OF LIVING
GILBERT ROHDE

RESIDENTIAL FURNITURE
TO SERVE A MORE MOBILE SOCIETY

"THERE SHOULD BE UTTER SIMPLICITY: NO SURFACE
ENRICHMENT, NO CARVINGS, NO MOLDINGS.... USING THE
BEST MATERIALS FOR THE JOB.... NOTHING SHOULD CRY
FOR ATTENTION."

In July 1930, furniture designer Gilbert Rohde introduced himself to D.J. De Pree, owner and president of Herman Miller, Inc. Outlining his design philosophy, Rohde informed De Pree that the furniture his company was producing was inappropriate for the times. Rohde held the view that furniture should not be the dominant physical characteristic of a space, but rather should serve the needs of people in that space.

PREVIOUS SPREAD

LEFT: **1933** Selner grey ash and mahogany in herringbone pattern
RIGHT: **1939** Vanity with leather-lined leg hole

→ **1942** Palado Group

↓ **1933** Century of Progress House catalog page

↑ **1940** East India Laurel Group bookcases pushed next to an L-shaped sectional

➡ **1940** Quarterfoil-shaped table from Palado Group with leather-wrapped legs

Rohde's furniture designs anticipated what has since been referred to as "a new scheme of living." Rohde was influenced by the Bauhaus style evolving in Europe, which was concerned with a refinement of materials, a simplification of design and greater function. Rohde approached his designs considering space saving issues and the utilitarian function of each piece. Rohde's observations and considerations of the change in the way people were living drove his designs.

GILBERT ROHDE
Herman Miller Designer

Gilbert Rohde, born in 1894, followed a very logical path to his career as a designer. He received a conventional education (which included training in the manual arts) in the Bronx and held several jobs before he became a furniture illustrator for a number of New York stores. Later, he traveled to Paris to see European designers and their design developments firsthand.

There, Rohde saw the work of avant-garde designers employing innovative materials to create unusual furniture forms. Returning to the United States, he coupled his impressions from Paris with his own distaste for superfluous detailing and his realization that Americans were going to be living in smaller spaces and moving more often. The result: a simplified style of furniture design, which employed new constructing techniques and deleted the need for excessive molding, expensive veneers, and applied carving to cover up poor craftsmanship.

—from the Herman Miller Archives, 1989

Rohde had recognized that American lifestyles were shifting. As people moved from rural communities to cities, more and more apartment buildings were constructed. Families traded the family farmhouse for a small apartment and a more transient lifestyle. Rohde also noted a lack of appropriately scaled and highly flexible furniture for this new style of living.

De Pree, whose company had been quickly devastated by the Depression, was persuaded that Rohde was onto something and that his ideas might provide a new future for Herman Miller. While initially uncomfortable with the dramatically different look of the furniture, De Pree liked its efficiency, clean lines, smaller proportions, honest use of materials, and adaptability.

Rohde suggested that Herman Miller pay him $1,000 per furniture drawing, a fee De Pree immediately rejected. Rohde then offered to work for a 3 percent royalty to be paid after the furniture sold. De Pree saw this as sound business and they proceeded.

As De Pree recalled years later in an oral history, "Some weeks later, we received our first drawings from Gilbert Rohde. I thought they looked as if they had been done in a manual training school and told him so. 'Eye Value' had become very important in selling. Rohde replied with a letter explaining why he designed the way he did. For his designs, there should be utter simplicity: no surface enrichment, no carvings, no moldings. This brought the necessity of precision. We would not cover up with moldings and carvings. He wrote about using the best materials for the job; he used chrome tubing where it was structurally better for the purpose. Nothing should cry for attention."

Rohde's designs focused on meeting needs with a clean aesthetic and functional flexibility. He created and introduced such now-standard pieces as multi-storage cabinets and sectional sofas. He used clear plastic for tabletops and legs. His upholstered furniture was characterized by smooth lines. The shapes were simple and unembellished. On the heels of the Art Déco period, he established the beginnings of mid-century modern furniture. Initially slow to sell, Rohde's furniture eventually began to get noticed. The sales catalogs for the line showed how to arrange the furniture and offered suggestions for adding modern furniture into a more traditional home.

Rohde's intent was to emphasize that the person was the most important element in a room. He encouraged the use of people in marketing photographs. While all photography of his designs and showrooms did not incorporate people, those that did helped present a style and sophistication uncommon to other furniture manufacturers of the time.

→ TOP LEFT: **1934** Living room with East India laurel bookcases

TOP RIGHT: **1939** Bedroom vanity

BOTTOM: **1939** Overstuffed chaise with glass table and tube legs

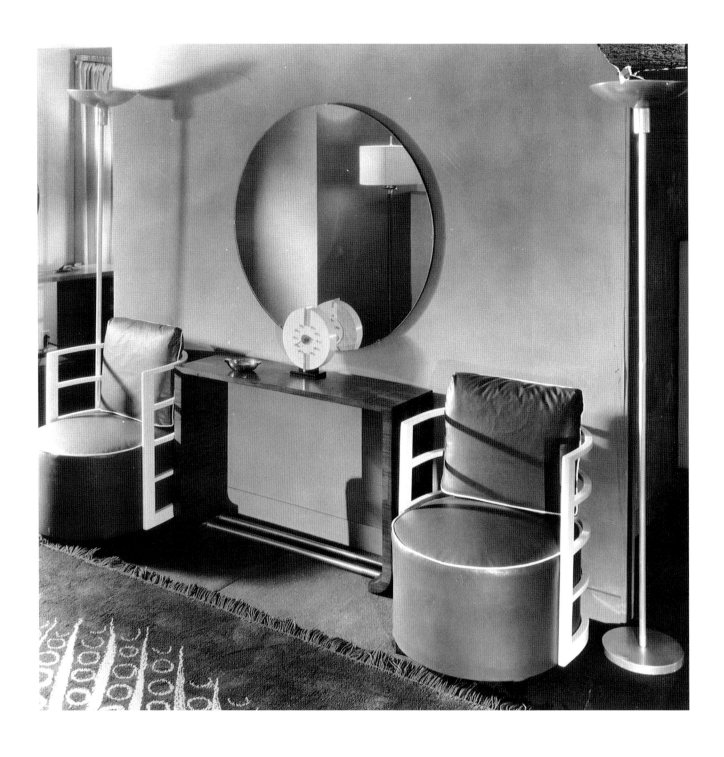

circa 1940 Dining console table from East
India Laurel Group

1942 Easy chair with matching ottoman
at the Keeler Building showroom

1942 Rohde Blueprint Group

Rohde's design for tables and chairs, how they work together as groupings and the common visual appeal of each piece provided an influence that can be seen in subsequent work by future Herman Miller designers. The utilitarian approach to design set the tone for Herman Miller's on-going concern of the identification of a need before designing a solution. The utilitarian nature of a bedroom was in stark contrast to the boudoir characteristics more typical of previous bedroom settings by Herman Miller and other furniture makers of the time.

1939 Vanity with mirror

De Pree recognized this time as the major turning point for Herman Miller and the beginnings of the designer as more than a stylist. In later remembrances, De Pree said, "Gilbert Rohde wrote that furniture should be anonymous. People are important, not furniture. Furniture should be useful. The room is primary. It must be planned for the people who are to live there. He was thinking about people. As a result, the furniture was space-saving, utilitarian, multipurpose."

In his book *Business as Unusual*, D.J. De Pree's oldest son, Hugh De Pree, a long-time president of the company, summarized Rohde's contribution: "Gilbert Rohde elevated our way of thinking from merely selling furniture to selling a way of life."

1942 Radio cabinet next to an easy chair

↑ **1942** Leather-wrapped storage cabinet

→ **1934** Chest and mirror combination of speckled
   wormwood with mirror off to the side. Also shown
   is a fluted chair and a cylindrical vanity bench.

PLACES WHERE STORAGE WALL COULD GO in an average home are shown in this drawing. On the first floor are the kitchen-dining-room storage wall and hall-living-room wall. On the second floor in the master bedroom (*left*) is a right-angled storage wall with a rad[io] and desk. In boys' room bookshelves as well as dresser are built into the storage wa[ll]

STORAGE WALL CAN BE USED ANYWHERE IN A HOM[E]

The color picture on the opposite page shows the great clutter of articles which can be kept neatly classified in shallow spaces of the storage wall. For lack of a good place to keep such things, families now cram them into bedroom closets along with vacuum cleaners, overcoats and suitcases. LIFE's living-room-hall storage wall is probably the most useful for the aver-

age home since it provides general storage space right in the middle of the house for miscellaneous, much-used things.

But the storage wall is a very flexible device. As the drawing above shows, it can be used almost anywhere to simplify the storage problem and to save space. Installed between the dining room and kitchen, it would eliminate the ordi-

nary sideboard and allow for a larger dining-roo[m] table. Between two bedrooms it would provid[e] built-in drawers and shelves and do away with [a] bulky dresser in each room. If a family ul[ti]mately had all the interior walls of its house bu[ilt] as storage walls it could buy all the clothes an[d] gadgets and knickknacks it wanted without ru[n]ning out of space in which to keep all of the[m]

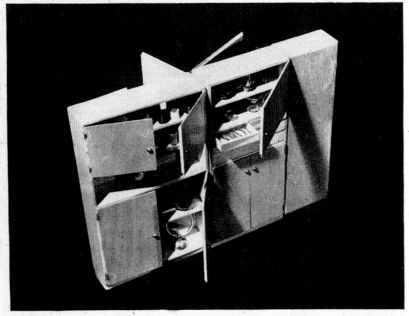

DINING-ROOM-KITCHEN STORAGE WALL would look like this model. Drawers for silver slide through wall. Knives and forks could be put in on kitchen side, taken out in dining room.

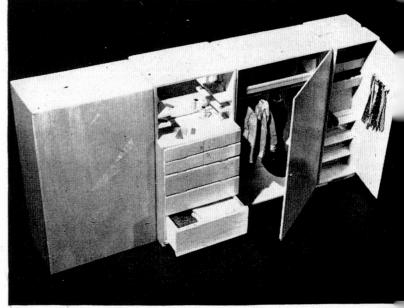

STORAGE WALL BETWEEN BEDROOMS would be 32 in. thick but would eliminate the re[gu]lar closets. Each side of the wall would have a space-saving, built-in dresser and mirr[or]

ELEVATING DESIGN
TO A FUNDAMENTAL
CORPORATE STRATEGY

"THE AVERAGE MANUFACTURER HAS NO CONVICTIONS
WHATEVER ABOUT DESIGN, OR ANY UNDERSTANDING
OF IT."

George Nelson was an architect, visionary, author, editor, and critic. But he is remembered today primarily as an industrial designer. He saw the world as a place to understand real problems and resolve them. The decline of American cities and his admiration for the way European cities were not overrun with cars led to his early concept of urban pedestrian malls, which he called "putting grass on Main Street." His desire for economical, efficient housing for returning veterans spawned his famed "storagewalls"—storage units built into the walls between rooms. They were approximately 12 inches deep—thicker than standard walls, but not as deep as closets—and since they provided storage for household goods, they rendered storage furniture, such as cabinets, chests, and bookshelves, unnecessary, and allowed more efficient, more flexible use of floor space. Nelson's storagewall concept was first published in *Architectural Forum*, then in *Life* magazine, and in Nelson's book, *Tomorrow's House*. Like Rohde before him, Nelson was not content to design furniture; he was conceiving entirely new lifestyles. Nelson's ideas caught the attention of D.J. De Pree, who noted that Nelson "is actively working on the things that will make for better living" and decided to hand him the design reins of Herman Miller.

PREVIOUS SPREAD

LEFT: **1994** Reintroduced platform bench

RIGHT: **1952** Basic storage cabinet at Max De Pree's home

← AND ↓ **1945** *Life* magazine

← **circa 1955** George Nelson with Irish setter

When Nelson accepted the position of Director of Design, he had never been inside a furniture manufacturing plant and had only dabbled in furniture design. His dabblings, however, were prophetic. He had already designed and fabricated a bench for his own office. The slat bench, which is still in production today, was intended to provide a place to pile materials and for visitors to sit briefly. Nelson didn't want the guest seating in his office to be too comfortable because he didn't want visitors to stay long. The slat bench met his own needs perfectly and later became part of his first collection of furniture for Herman Miller.

After accepting his new post, Nelson continued to live in New York and write for several publications. He convinced *Fortune* magazine that he should do a story on the furniture industry, complete with a national research tour of furniture-making facilities. From the tour, he learned much about furniture manufacturing and about the weaknesses of the casegoods industry. The resulting article, published in January 1947, was highly critical of the industry.

> Whenever furniture is criticized, the public is blamed. "When they want something better," runs the refrain, "We'll be only too glad to make it for them." The average manufacturer has no convictions whatever about design, or any understanding of it....
>
> The public, as always, buys what it is shown and does not clamor for things that do not exist.

He also criticized the power of the retailer, who, as the crucial middleman between the manufacturer and the customer, could refuse to stock styles he disliked. Thus, manufacturers were sure to keep retailers happy. Nelson saw that the relationship between furniture manufacturer, dealer, architect, interior designer, and the customer needed to be revamped, and began his campaign at Herman Miller to design a better way.

↑ **1994** Reintroduced platform bench

→ **1946** Slatted bench with basic cabinet hotel unit

↑ **circa 1948** Basic cabinet—hotel unit

Nelson's slat bench design, conceived before he joined Herman Miller, became both a logical and functional base for a series of case goods, which could use the bench independently or as a part of the construction. The numerous case goods Nelson designed each met a different need that George perceived, whether storage for office materials, household goods, books, papers or phonograph records each represented a particular use.

Nelson proclaimed, "There is a market for good design." In his first year with the company, he designed and introduced almost eighty pieces of furniture. The majority of those products were a modular system of simple casegoods made with minimal materials. The bench that he had designed for his own office formed a central part of the collection. It doubled as a base for the storage modules, which were available in numerous configurations—for example, with two drawers stacked, two drawers side-by-side, or three drawers.

His new knowledge of the industry provided insights into how a manufacturing company could produce quality products profitably. He had noticed that the successful companies had engineers on staff who shaped the design process, so he suggested that De Pree hire an engineer, which De Pree promptly did.

→ **circa 1947** Utility cabinet

4690

4691

4692

4693

Multi-purpose design is an accurate reflection of modern living conditions, for the mobility of the average family makes versatility a highly desirable characteristic of its furniture. The platform bench, shown here, is primarily a high base for deep and shallow cases, but it also serves as a low table and for extra seating. When used for the latter purpose it can be fitted with upholstered foam rubber cushions which are available in 24, 48 and 72 inch lengths (C-24, C-48, C-72). The standard finishes are Prima Vera finish on Birch with ebonized legs, or all ebonized.

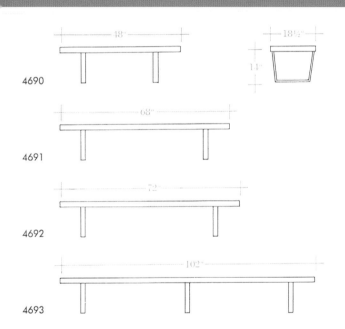

The Herman Miller Furniture Company announces a new group of household furniture designed by George Nelson, one of the leading U.S. exponents of modern design. The furniture will be introduced at the company's showrooms in Chicago, Los Angeles and New York shortly after the beginning of 1947

herman miller-zeeland-michigan

George Nelson

design

↑ **circa 1947** First use of logo in
advertisement for Nelson Designs

↓ Catalog cover

The Herman Miller logo was first intended to replace the 'M' in Miller. It became more of a stand-alone logo in subsequent years supported by the full spelling of the name. These early promotional graphics demonstrate how the now famous logo was first used. Recognized for its own shape, the logo is considered one of Americas graphic icons.

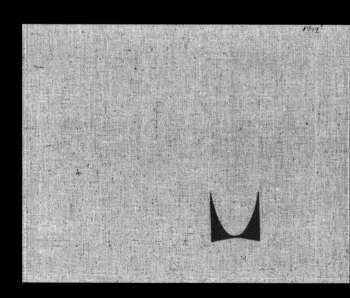

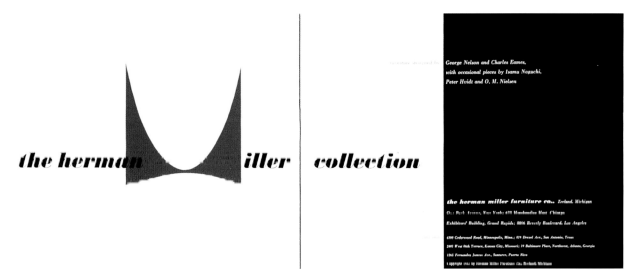

the herman **M** *iller* | *collection*

*George Nelson and Charles Eames,
with occasional pieces by Isamu Noguchi,
Peter Hvidt and O. M. Nielsen*

the herman miller furniture co., Zeeland, Michigan

On: Park Avenue, New York; 671 Merchandise Mart Chicago

Exhibitors' Building, Grand Rapids; 8806 Beverly Boulevard, Los Angeles

4309 Cedarwood Road, Minneapolis, Minn.; 419 Drexel Ave., San Antonio, Texas

2401 West 86th Terrace, Kansas City, Missouri; 19 Baltimore Place, Northwest, Atlanta, Georgia

1265 Fernandez Juncos Ave., Santurce, Puerto Rico

Copyright 1952 by Herman Miller Furniture Co., Zeeland, Michigan

1952 Catalog title page with stylized M logo

His design efforts went far beyond the products. In many ways, George Nelson designed the Herman Miller company itself. He certainly raised design to a corporate strategy. He believed that in order to earn a reputation for quality products, all the public elements of the company, particularly those that included the consumer, must represent quality too. This led him to create a consistent image for Herman Miller's printed pieces, including stationery and catalogs. His office designed a logo, prescribed typographic usage, and dictated graphic style. His logo, still used today, was a stylized M. (For more on graphic design at Herman Miller, see chapter 7.)

He created displays that showed customers the products in a realistic environment, which allowed them to visualize the pieces in their own homes. Showrooms, which had been arranged as rows upon rows of furniture, were redesigned as vignettes of living rooms and bedrooms—a much more suggestible selling approach. Although the showrooms were strictly "for the trade," meaning that only architects and interior designers were invited, sometimes those professionals brought their clients in to see particular items.

Nelson recruited other designers to Herman Miller who went on to change the face of design—and turn the company into a design powerhouse. He seemed to have an intuitive sense of designers who mattered and who would define a company with their style. He recruited Isamu Noguchi, Charles and Ray Eames, and Alexander Girard. With numerous talented designers, working collaboratively and separately, Herman Miller's deep commitment to design itself was fully represented. It also gave them a tremendous competitive edge. Noguchi created lamps and tables in organic materials and shapes. Girard, known for his vivid colors and patterns, created Herman Miller's textiles department. The Eameses, of course, were responsible for many of the company's most iconic and enduring designs.

4672 vanity stool, with upholstered spring and foam rubber cushion on an aluminum frame.

4698 upholstered stool for bed or dressing room. Leg design matches vanity 4660.

4676 large ottoman, which, used in conjunction with the upholstered chairs, creates luxurious reclining pieces. Ideal for comfortable extra seating.

The effect of Nelson's innovations cannot be overstated. When he came on board, Herman Miller sales were less than $500,000. Within 4 years, they rose to $1.2 million, and in less than 7 years were over $3 million. The company had 120 employees when he started, and after the Eameses came on board, approximately 600 people were on the payroll.

In the 1948 sales catalog, written and designed by Nelson's office, Nelson summed up the company's design philosophy, which of course he had devised—and which is still relevant today: "1. What you make is important. 2. Design is an integral part of the business. 3. The product must be honest. 4. You decide what you will make. 5. There is a market for good design."

← **1949** Catalog page

↓ **circa 1950** Basic cabinet—residential

1950 Nelson sectional seating in showroom display

While the concept of the sectional sofa is attributed to Rohde it was Nelson who converted that concept into more rectangular shapes with increased options for flexibility. Nelson's designs for sofas, tables, and chairs had a compatible aesthetic and a common sense of utility. Nelson's desk design recognized the importance of accommodating the way a person worked before the concept of ergonomics existed. These desks take into consideration the need for easily accessible filing, storage, and location for typewriters, phones, and office support materials of the day.

1956 Desk with flip open typing table

← **1958** Pretzel chair in front of a
rosewood cabinet

↑ **circa 1968** Single pedestal desk with
woven screen and cube group chair

1965 Elkins Shoe Store, Boston, Massachusetts, using Nelson seating and storage with hanging lamps covered in Girard fabric and Eames walnut stools.

2000 Reintroduced Herman Miller for the Home marshmallow sofa

The Marshmallow Sofa, an icon of mid-century modern design, could be called a design failure. An inventor presented the Nelson Office with examples of his ability to produce a round foam disc that became "self-skinned." The Nelson Office recognized that the discs' low cost and high resiliency suggested the potential for mass-produced, inexpensive seating. They developed a prototype of a sofa with discs on a frame and presented it to Herman Miller management, who readily approved. As full-scale production was planned, however, it became obvious that the material did not live up to the inventor's promise. But because the appearance of the proposed sofa was so intriguing, Herman Miller and the Nelson Office worked on a solution. The only one found used upholstered foam discs and required extensive hand labor. Not low cost seating, from its introduction, the Marshmallow Sofa was a luxury item.

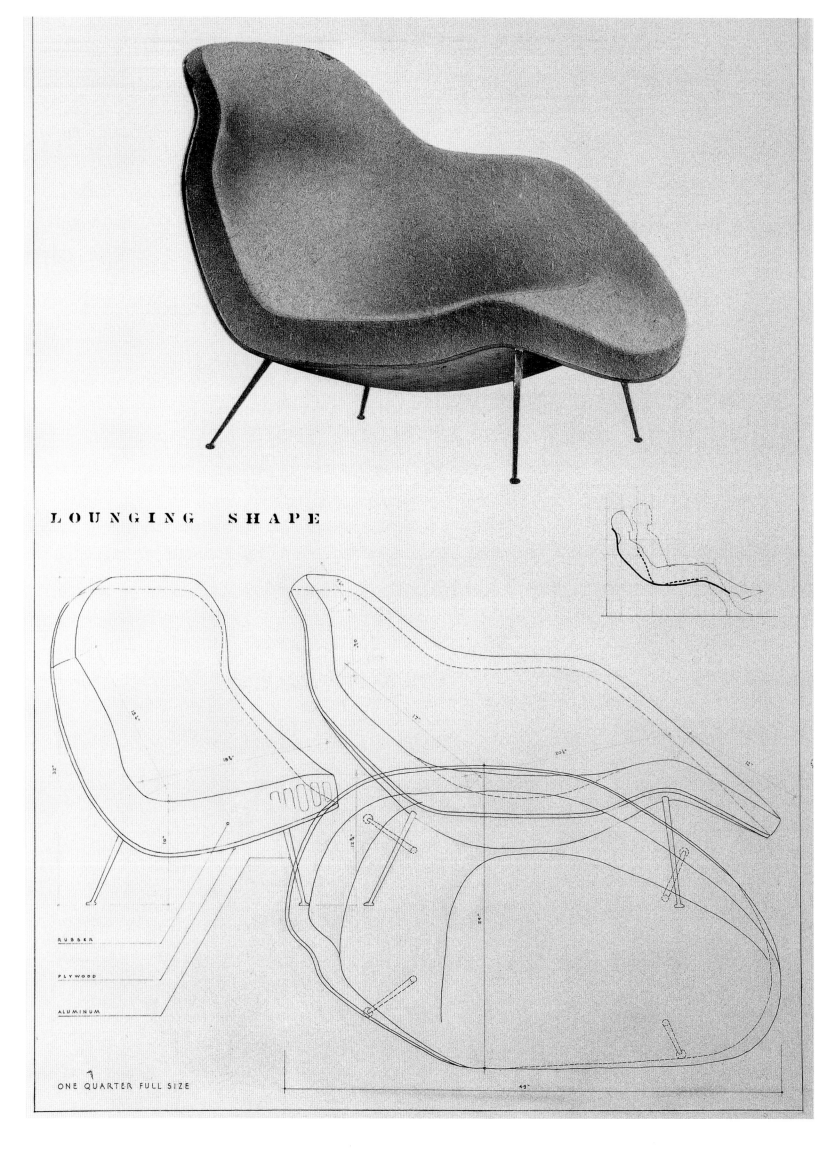

LOUNGING SHAPE

RUBBER

PLYWOOD

ALUMINUM

ONE QUARTER FULL SIZE

CHAPTER 3

NEW MATERIALS AND PROCESSES
CHARLES AND RAY EAMES

AN INEXPENSIVE, HIGH-QUALITY CHAIR

THE EAMESES' DESIGNS FOR SEATING WERE DEDICATED TO THE IDEA OF COMFORT.

The legendary design duo of Charles and Ray Eames met at Cranbrook Academy of Art, in Michigan, in 1940. Charles Eames, an architect, was co-director, with Eero Saarinen, of the school's industrial design department. Ray Kaiser came to Cranbrook as a student after studying painting in New York with Hans Hofmann. They first worked together later that year, when Ray and fellow student Harry Bertoia helped Charles and Saarinen with the preparation of their entry for "Organic Design in Home Furnishings," a design competition sponsored by the Museum of Modern Art (MoMA) in New York. The team's proposed designs involved two new manufacturing techniques: molding plywood and cycle-welding rubber to wood. The entry included molded-wood chairs, a sectional sofa, and benches, cabinets, desks, and tables formed by a modular system—all shown in handmade prototypes and presentation drawings. Some of the wood chairs were covered with padding and upholstery; others were left uncovered.

PREVIOUS SPREAD

LEFT: 1948 Drawing by Charles Eames and Eero Saarinen that took first place in the Organic Design in Home Furnishing Competition

RIGHT: circa 1947 LCM chairs with a variety of woods and finishes

← **1969** Charles and Ray Eames

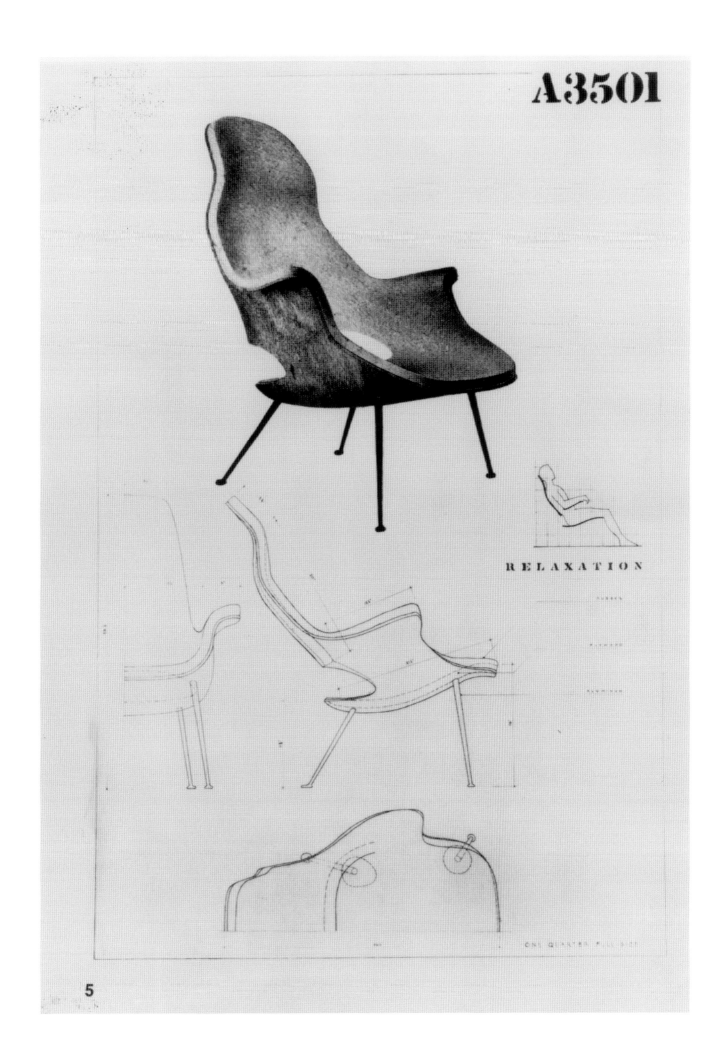

A3501

RELAXATION

5

The Eames-Saarinen entry won first place in two categories, Seating and Case Goods for a Living Room. Charles was immediately a recognized designer, and Ray his trusted teammate.

Charles and Ray married in 1941 and moved to California, where they pursued various interests, from graphics to set design and filmmaking. The MoMA competition had sparked their interest in molded plywood as a modern material for everyday furniture. They were determined to create an economical, mass-produced chair of molded plywood.

No manufacturing process existed for molded plywood, so they needed to design and develop all aspects of production. They struggled to understand the complex issues of laminating various wood plies, how they should be glued together, and how to create compound curves that were structurally sound. Working in their apartment, they built what they called the "Kazam" machine—their experimental device for molding plywood. They used it to test full-size prototypes, greatly preferring three-dimensional models to drawings. Unfortunately for their neighbors, however, the Kazam frequently blew out the power in their building.

↑ **1941** Kazam machine built by Charles and Ray in their Los Angeles apartment to experiment with molding plywood

→ **1942** Splints developed for the Navy—Charles Eames's leg was used for the mold

A doctor friend visiting from St. Louis told them about wounded soldiers in World War II being further injured during transport because the metal splints amplified the vibrations of the stretcher. Intrigued, the Eameses began to design and develop a molded plywood splint.

In the splint development process they learned a great deal about how plywood worked. They learned that if the grain of each layer was perpendicular to the layer below, the moldability and strength of the wood increased. They found that the wood was less likely to break where it was bent if openings were cut into the wood at the bends—and that those openings could double as handles or places to secure bandages. They took their finished design to the Navy, who made an initial order of 5,000, but eventually 150,000 were used.

As the war ended and the need for splints ceased, Charles and Ray were able to apply the lessons of the splints to their original problem of chairs. They gave up on creating a seat-and-back out of one piece of plywood, realizing that even if it could be achieved it would be too expensive, and focused instead on creating separate pieces.

↓ **1949** Catalog page

L C M

Low Chair — Metal.
Birch, walnut, calico ash, black, red.

26¾"

15¾"

25"

In 1945, the Eameses introduced their molded-plywood lounge chair (known as LCW) and dining chair (DCW)—which were both functional and beautiful. The chairs were produced by Evans Products, a manufacturer based in Venice, California, who was used to working with wood. The Eameses had worked with Evans to create the tooling that would mold plywood in the same way they had done it in their apartment.

At first the chairs were slow to catch on, and the Evans Company suggested a small press and trade preview of the furniture at the Barclay Hotel in New York. The preview, which opened in December 1945, succeeded in attracting attention. It was at the Barclay that George Nelson first saw the Eameses' work, and decided to recruit them to Herman Miller.

Evans, a West Coast company with extremely limited distribution, welcomed Herman Miller's involvement. At first, Herman Miller distributed the chairs that Evans produced, but eventually they bought the wood-molding division of Evans altogether. Herman Miller launched the Eames chairs in 1946—the same year that they were

→ **1946** Molded plywood chair with screw-attached shock mounts connecting back to base frame

The investigation of how to mold plywood into complex compound curves brought the realization that a chair was most efficiently designed by using molded components which were then connected with "forgiving" shock mounts. This recognition of how to connect independently molded parts gave rise to the molded plywood chair introduced in 1946, and was recognized by *Time Magazine* in 2000 as the most significant design of the twentieth century.

1946 The LCW chair in red plywood

1994 Herman Miller for the Home
molded-plywood coffee table

included in a small exhibition at MoMA, the museum's first one-man furniture show, called *New Furniture Designed by Charles Eames.* Since their launch, the chairs have never been out of production, and in January 2000, *Time* magazine named the molded-plywood lounge chair (LCW) the "best design of the twentieth century."

Charles and Ray Eames's collaboration with Herman Miller would last more than forty years. After the LCW and DCW, it would expand to include new versions with metal legs, tables and storage units, classroom seating, airport seating, and stackable chairs. There were experiments with new materials—fiberglass and plastics—and new manufacturing processes. Infinitely creative, the Eameses were always curious and always experimenting.

In addition to molding plywood, the Eameses studied the then-new material, fiberglass, and developed the method for molding fiberglass into seating. The resulting chairs became widely used in environments that required easy-to-clean, stackable, light-weight chairs, such as schools, offices, and auditoriums. In the early 1990s, Herman Miller and the Eames family decided to cease production of the fiberglass shells because fiberglass is not recyclable. Since then, Herman Miller and the Eames office found a new material meeting the concerns of sustainability and recyclability while maintaining the intentions of the first design. Reintroduced in 2001, the plastic chair shell by authorization by the Eames family remains authentic.

2000 Molded plywood LCW in ebony

circa 1960 Molded fiberglass
stacking shell chairs

2000 Eames lounge and ottoman in walnut

The Eameses first started thinking about a cushioned lounge chair in the mid-1940s, one with, in Charles's words, the "warm, receptive look of a well-used first baseman's mitt." They tried several times to design an all-plywood frame, creating one of interlocking molded-plywood pieces in 1946. Over the next ten years, the design was refined into the Lounge Chair and Ottoman, introduced in 1956. The lounge and ottoman combined molding technology with hand-craftsmanship, and has become an icon of quality, comfort, and mid-century design. Although frequently copied, the design now has trade-dress protection (a form of copyright for three-dimensional products), one of only a very few furniture designs to be granted such distinction.

↑ **1956** Stockbroker John Meyer, a friend of Charles's, posing in an Eames lounge chair for a Herman Miller advertisement

Eameses' designs for seating were dedicated to the idea of comfort. Their concern for adapting to body movement, support and forgiving edges preceded significant research in the areas of ergonomics. The Eames lounge chair introduced in 1956 evolved over a long period of time. Eameses' intention was to create a chair that would be an American "club chair" and provide the comfort as if "one were sitting in a well-worn catcher's mitt."

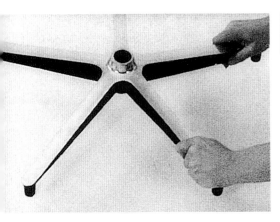
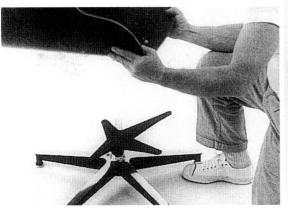
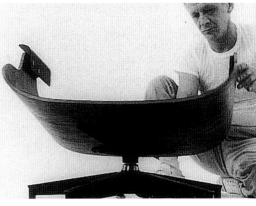

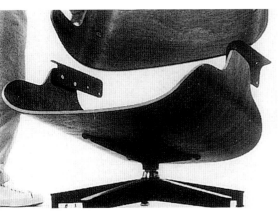

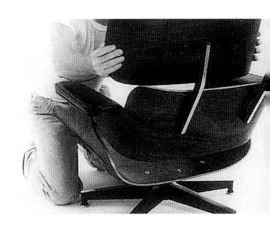

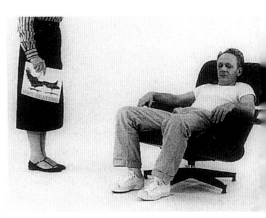

1956 Sequence of frames showing Dick Hoffman assembling the lounge chair. The frames were taken from 16mm film footage

A diversion from the Eameses' initial approach to create inexpensive mass-produced furniture, the use of the highest quality woods and hand sewn leather cushions went in the opposite direction. The assembly of the components was effectively shown in a short film the Eames' office produced to coincide with the public introduction of the chair on the *Arlene Francis Home Show* aired on NBC in 1956.

1946 Ray Eames in an early variation
of a plywood lounge chair

2000 An occupied Eames lounge and
ottoman at Marigold Lodge

1998 Herman Miller for the Home furniture
in the library at the Marigold Lodge

← **1960** Walnut stools designed by Ray Eames for the lobby of the Time Life building to serve as low tables or seats

The walnut stools are good examples of problem-solving. The Eames Office was hired to design the lobby spaces of the Time Life Building at Rockefeller Center in New York City. The spaces were used by visitors during the day, and, in the evenings, as break areas for pressmen. The Eameses created special seating, now called the Time Life Chair, and these stools, which were meant to serve as both an accompanying table and additional seating.

They started with a cube and began to reduce the visual mass with angular cuts, but the resulting shapes were not pleasing, so next they tried turning a cube in a lathe—which produced more welcoming shapes. With several profiles developed, they chose these three for production. Black walnut was chosen for its hardness and durability. Ray Eames shared that the hardest part of designing the stool was determining the right depression for the top so that it could hold a glass and be comfortable for sitting. A need identified, a solution provided.

1960 Time Life chair with walnut stools

HIGH-QUALITY INDOOR-OUTDOOR FURNITURE

THE RECENT INTRODUCTION OF A MESH ON ALUMINUM GROUP CHAIRS BRINGS THE ORIGINAL DESIGN BACK FULL CIRCLE.

While working with Eero Saarinen and Alexander Girard on a house for Irwin Miller, founder of Cummins Engines, in Columbus, Indiana, the Eameses designed a set of chairs originally called the Leisure Group or the Indoor-Outdoor Group (later renamed the Aluminum Group). The collection, introduced in 1958, was designed as high-quality outdoor furniture.

They first conceived of a seat frame to support stretched fabric. They designed structural side members in cast aluminum that had a groove along their length that would allow fabric to be inserted. A strip of cordlike material was sewn into the fabric, and then, similar to the way a painter stretches canvas over a frame, it was fed into the groove in the side pieces. The fabric of the original chairs was a synthetic mesh (woven saran).

The two side members were connected by two cast aluminum stretchers serving dual functions. The top stretcher doubles as a handle for moving the chair, and the bottom stretcher, dubbed "the antler," connects the seat to the pedestal base. Although the original chair is the centerpiece, the collection also includes a high-backed chair, an ottoman, and office chairs. And in 1969, the Soft Pad Group was developed. Using the same frame and fabric-attachment method, plush cushions were added.

← **2002** National Design Center Eames aluminum chair with a walnut stool

↓ **2001** Aluminum Group chairs with black mesh

Side

Executive

Management

← **1958** Back view of the aluminum group chair production model

➡ **1958** Don Albinson inserting Royalite strip into upholstery

➡ **1958** Charles and the "antler" seat section and base pedestal

Charles and Ray both worked to create almost sculptural-like visual appeal to functional items. The method of working involved the creation of three-dimensional prototypes with numerous iterations to get to the "just right shape" that satisfied the purpose while meeting their aesthetic needs. The first aluminum group chair designed for the Irwin Miller house in Columbus, Indiana, incorporated a woven mesh saran material. The saran mesh was unable to accommodate a long-term use. The mesh was discontinued at the time due to its limited wear ability. The recent introduction of a mesh on aluminum group chairs brings the original design back full circle. The continuing collaboration between Herman Miller and the Eames family keeps the design authentic. New technology and previously nonexistent materials allow for the intial intent of including mesh material to be met.

Designers today often refer to an "Eames style" or say that something is "Eamesian." This usually means simple components and minimal materials to meet a clear need. In reality, the Eameses did not have a style. Instead, each product is a unique response to the problem at hand.

Common to all the products designed by Charles and Ray Eames are the honest use of materials, careful consideration of how one material connects to another, and attention to detail. Charles often said, "The details are not the details, they are the product." They are also highly functional. Ray said, "What works is better than what looks good, " and the Eames pieces manage to do both.

← **1958** Charles and Ray examining the sling locations to be covered by fabric lapping

→ **circa 1946** Molded plywood chair

CHAPTER 4 : **A DESIGN FOR PARTICIPATION**
THE SCANLON PLAN

A MANAGEMENT PHILOSOPHY THAT ENCOURAGES PROBLEM-SOLVING

DESIGN IS NOT LIMITED TO CREATING TANGIBLE ITEMS. IT IS ALSO POSSIBLE TO DESIGN A PROCESS.

In the early 1950s, Herman Miller adopted a management program called the Scanlon Plan. Conceived by Joseph Scanlon, a steelworker and union leader in the 1930s, and refined by Professor Carl Frost of Michigan State University, it fostered a cooperative and mutually respectful attitude between labor and management.

Early in his leadership of the company, D.J. De Pree had been deeply affected by the death of a millwright who worked for him. The millwright was a key plant position at the time, responsible for operating the steam-powered woodmill. When he visited the millwright's family to pay his respects, the widow read some poetry, which he liked very much. To De Pree's surprise, the poetry had been written by the millwright. The realization that his employees had their own creative pursuits and hidden dreams had a strong effect on De Pree. He became determined to create an environment that would enable employees to flourish.

In 1950, several members of Herman Miller's management team read an article on the Scanlon Plan in the January issue of *Fortune* magazine. The Scanlon Plan aims to create organizational effectiveness while promoting individual growth and responsibility. Four principles form its core: identity, participation, equity, and competence. Identity centers around the individual's value, and the belief that how a person is treated affects his or her performance. Participation is how the employees and management interact; management offers employees the opportunity to influence decisions in their area of expertise, and employees accept that responsibility. Equity is the balance of management and labor interests (along with those of customers, investors, and other constituents); it includes profit-sharing and open-book management. Finally, competence requires constant improvement and enlargement through training and increased responsibility.

Shortly thereafter, Dr. Carl Frost was the featured speaker at a meeting sponsored by the Grand Rapids Manufacturers Association. The conference only increased Herman Miller's interest in adopting the Scanlon Plan, and subsequent meetings were arranged.

When Dr. Frost met with management, he pointed out that the Scanlon Plan is not a static set of mandates imposed on a company. Rather, it is a fluid set of principles that each company must tailor to its own mission and identity. Fundamentally, however, it required sharing a lot of information about the business with employees and an acceptance

PREVIOUS SPREAD

A Scanlon indices page used

to track monthly performance

↑ CEO Max De Pree addressing

a monthly Scanlon meeting

(circa 1982)

A Scanlon work-team information meeting,
reporting corporate performance and gathering
questions for subsequent answers (circa 1983)

of change and growth as continuous conditions. Herman Miller's management team agreed, and adopted this new process.

At Herman Miller, an organizational structure that brought workers and management closer together via open communication had the added benefit of revealing company problems and encouraging solutions from anyone. Joseph Scanlon and Carl Frost were both designers, although they would not have thought of themselves that way. They designed a communication and management process that allowed for problems to be openly shared and resolved collectively.

For many years, Scanlon meetings were held monthly at Herman Miller to share information widely throughout the corporation. These meetings were led by senior management and attended by representatives of the various divisions of the corporation. Designers often attended these meetings to present their products and the ideas behind them. The representatives then took information back to their work teams, and recorded any resulting questions and any solutions to problems raised in the meetings. Most important to making this process work was a deep commitment on both sides to open communication. Employees were free to raise even the most contentious issues with management, and instead of fearing reprisal, they knew their input would be respected and even appreciated.

While working at Herman Miller, I got to see the Scanlon Plan in action firsthand. During my first meeting, several hundred people were listening to the president, CEO, and other senior officers talk about the market, production, products, and financial performance. The person sitting next to me, whom I had only just met, stood up during the question period and said, pointedly, "The company stock has gone down two points, and I want to know why and what you are going to do to fix it." Thinking I had sat next to the corporate nut, I felt embarrassed, and it was to my great surprise that the president replied, "Great question, let me tell you what we know about that, what we think is the reason, and what we are going to be doing about it."

Open communication extended beyond that between management and labor. Different departments of labor were also open with each other. Designers might visit a manufacturing floor to make sure that a product was being made to the specifications. At the same time, someone on the production floor could offer suggestions for how to improve a product.

Today, the Scanlon Plan has evolved into a communication process that aligns the economic value added (EVA) through tracked performance.

The Scanlon Plan, its use at Herman Miller for decades, and the EVA program, demonstrate that design is not limited to creating tangible items. It is also possible to design a process—using the problem-solving ethos—to identify challenges and opportunities for the company at large. Through truly open, two-way communication in corporate meetings, creative problem-solving is applied to management to help the company maximize its potential.

CHAPTER 5 : **WHITE-COLLAR WORKERS**
ACTION OFFICE AND ROBERT PROPST

↑ **1964** Action Office 1 with desk, storage carrel, stand-up work surface, and communications carrel

PREVIOUS SPREAD

LEFT: **1964** Action Office 1 freestanding units, in an enclosed space

RIGHT: **1979** Action Office installation at Batt's Building, Zeeland, Michigan

A FLEXIBLE OFFICE SYSTEM
FOR MODERN WORK

"OUR FIRST DIRECTIVE...WAS TO FIND PROBLEMS OUTSIDE
OF THE FURNITURE INDUSTRY..."

circa 1985 Robert Propst

The Herman Miller company never explicity set out to conceive a whole new way of working. But that's exactly what they did when they introduced an open office system in 1964—a product that grew out of the Research Division (later the Herman Miller Research Corporation), which the company established in 1960, under the direction of Robert Propst.

Propst had first studied chemical engineering in college, but after he took one design course, he switched his major to art. However, he never called himself a designer. Instead, he thought of himself as a researcher studying large problems in a changing world. He went back to school at the University of Colorado for his master's degree and headed a branch of the university's art department. He would say later, "I really had a good time teaching. ... And then, I developed the idea—and this finally became a passion—that the artist needed to be more involved functionally in society."

D.J. De Pree met Propst in 1958 while visiting his son John in Boulder, Colorado. He asked an architect friend of John's if anyone in the area was doing interesting work. The friend named Robert Propst, who had opened a small architecture-sculpture business in Denver. De Pree was immediately taken with Propst and his great interest in research. De Pree encouraged another of his sons, Hugh, then president of Herman Miller, to meet with Propst.

Hugh was keen to see Herman Miller diversify beyond furniture. During his discussions with Propst, the idea for a research institution developed. Hugh De Pree later wrote, "Our first directive to [Propst] was to find problems outside of the furniture industry and to conceive solutions for them. He immediately began flooding us with ideas, concepts, and drawings ranging from agriculture to medicine. It is interesting, though, that despite our mutual desire to explore other fields, the first project that attracted his continuing attention was the office and as early as 1960 he began outlining his concepts for this activity."

As the Research Corporation's facility was being built in Ann Arbor, Michigan, Propst was displeased with the furniture provided. He found the freestanding case goods (from other Herman Miller lines) too rigid for a research space, which would need to continually adapt to new projects and assignments. He also believed white-collar

OVERLEAF

1968 Action Office, JFN Chicago

1969 Early Action Office 2 installation with Eames shell chairs and woman seated on Eames compact sofa

work of all kinds required an environment that was flexible and responsive to new ideas and changing opportunities. However, Propst knew little about the dynamics of white-collar work.

To correct this informational void and using his usual in-depth research, Propst set out to understand the workings of an office. He met not just with office users, interior designers, and architects, but also with social psychologists, behavioral psychologists, mathematicians, and many others. Armed with information about how offices physically support knowledge work, he set about creating a series of products to serve the workplace. During the 1950s, American industry was booming. The end of the war and the rise in consumer goods, such as cars and televisions, meant that many companies needed much more space. With traditional offices, they had to move or renovate—options that were expensive, disruptive, and permanent. Propst's idea for a flexible wall system installed in a large, open space would change all that. Propst came up with a concept and a plan, George Nelson gave them physical form. The result was Action Office 1, introduced in 1964—the world's first modular office system. The products, although attractive, were cumbersome and not especially easy to move. The design was refined and relaunched in a second generation called Action Office 2 in 1967.

The concept of interlocking wall panels, work surfaces, and storage raised off the ground was immediately lauded in the press. However, few architects and interior designers understood how to use it.

A marketing campaign meant to educate design professionals about this new system was created. It included the creation of an educational demonstration center and presentations around the country on the changing trends of office work. Sales of Action

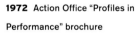

1972 Action Office "Profiles in Performance" brochure

⬆ **1972** Action Office with Eames chairs and Girard fabrics

Action Office met an office facility need and demonstrated learning from Herman Miller predecessors. Rohde's concern for the individual, Eames's concern for materials, Nelson's concern for flexibility can all be seen as influences to the development of Action Office. Propst's concern for the issues of health, function and facility met the needs of white-collar work in the '60s. Still available today, Action Office is continually updated to accommodate the ever-changing needs for electronics, data, and space utilization.

↑ **1988** Action Office Encore

The office
A facility based
on change

By Robert Propst

Office 1 and 2 were slow until a competitor created a similar product and validated the concept. From that point on, a phenomenon was born and grew to a multibillion-dollar industry. Propst's research was documented in his book *A Facility Based on Change* (1968), which became the definitive document on how modern offices work, the benefits of and need to adapt to an ever-changing world.

As Propst has stated (Yvonne Abraham, "The Man Behind the Cubicle" *Metropolis,* November 1998), he was trying to encourage movement: "It's truly amazing the number of decisive events and critical dialogues that occur when people are out of their seated, stuffy contexts, and moving around chatting with each other." He went on to say, "The Action Office was supposed to be invisible and embellished with identity and communication artifacts and whatever you needed to create individuation.... We wanted this to be the vehicle to carry other expressions of identity. That's why we provided tackboards and all kinds of display surfaces." But he realizes what has become of his high ideal in most offices. "Not all organizations are intelligent and progressive. Lots are run by crass people who can take the same kind of equipment and create hellholes. They make little bitty cubicles and stuff people in them." While Dilbert cartoonist Scott Adams later had appropriate fun with that problem, Herman Miller went on to see what they could do to address the issue (see Chapter 8—Facility Management).

OVERLEAF

1978 Action Office with Ergon chair

CHAPTER 6 : **ERGONOMICS**
BILL STUMPF

A HEALTHY, COMFORTABLE OFFICE CHAIR

THE CHAIR SHOULD PROVIDE A STRUCTURE WHICH WILL
REDUCE PHYSIOLOGICAL STRESS AND HELP MAINTAIN THE
HEALTH OF THE BODY.

In 1966 at the University of Wisconsin's Environmental Design Center, industrial designer Bill Stumpf began to intently study human factors and seating. Using an experimental chair that he had made, with changeable seats, backs, and arm-rests, he studied what was comfortable for people of widely different height, weight, and body proportions. He examined, with time-lapse photography, the movement and postures of office workers at their desks. He gathered data from orthopedists and vascular specialists on the physiological effects of seating. Stumpf took this initial research with him to the Herman Miller Research Corpora-tion, when he joined in 1968 and continued his work. In the early 1970s, he for-mulated a problem statement entitled "A Chair Is a Chair Is a Problem":

> Most of us work for organizations where we sit in an office at a desk, a conference table, or a CRT screen for extended and often uninterrupted periods of time. Seldom, however, do we ourselves select our own chair. Usually it has been spec-ified by someone else who has sat in it for a total of less than two minutes.
>
> Office environments typically emphasize interior design coherence rather than user coherence. Economic and other restraints often force the specifier to select seating which is not compatible with the human body.
>
> As a result, many of us spend eight hours a day in a chair that is uncomfort-able, that restricts our movement and inhibits our performance, and is causing us to suffer from a combination of vascular and postural problems. . . .

Stumpf then established four basic design criteria for chairs.

Comfort: Because people develop a mental set of what constitutes chair comfort, comfort is as much a matter of mind as it is of matter. The chair, therefore, should be perceived as comfortable before, during, and after sitting on it.

Task Motivating: Recognizing that sitting is only a means to another end, the chair should provide postural security in the variety of positions that a worker assumes in task performance.

PREVIOUS SPREAD

1992 Ergon with adjustable arms

→ **1996** Ergon management chairs taken at the Pavilion, Grandville, Michigan

↑ **1995** Bill Stumpf

← **circa 1984** Ergon

OVERLEAF

1996 Ergon management chairs with Liaison cabinets at the Grandville Pavilion in Grandville, Michigan

Accommodating: Since the chair will have to serve more than one individual, it should be designed so that it can be easily adjusted to fit most body sizes.

Health Giving: The chair should provide a structure that will reduce physiological stress and help maintain the health of the body.

In 1974, Herman Miller asked Stumpf to translate these criteria into a chair for office workers. The result was introduced two years later and derived its name, the Ergon chair, from ergonomics, the study of a person's relationship to the physical environment.

The Ergon chair was not an immediate success. Despite Stumpf's years of research, the chair was met with skepticism—perhaps because of its radical aesthetics. One potential customer remarked that it looked "like two hemorrhoid pillows put together to make a chair." As with the Action Office system, public education and a marketing campaign was needed.

Rather than just showing the chair alone or next to more traditional models, Herman Miller salespeople took time up front to educate customers on the potentially hazardous issues of long-term sitting. Once the problems were recognized and the Ergon's solutions evident, the chair was readily accepted and became both a functional and aesthetic example that many others soon followed.

Even today, after three decades and more ergonomic research, the Ergon chair, with a few adaptations along the way, continues to sell strongly. Stumpf's recognition of an unheralded need and his meticulous development of an appropriate product generated a new genre of seating and has provided health benefits for an untold number of office workers.

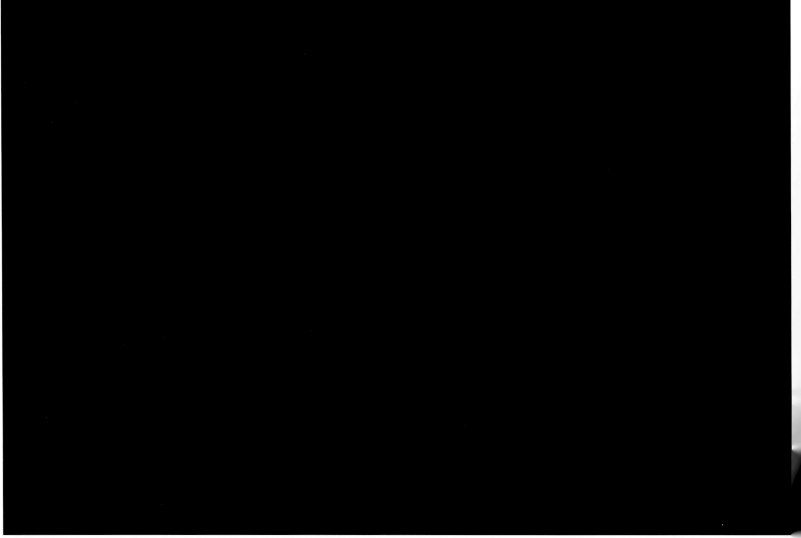

CHAPTER 7 : **WORDS, ACTIONS, POLICIES**

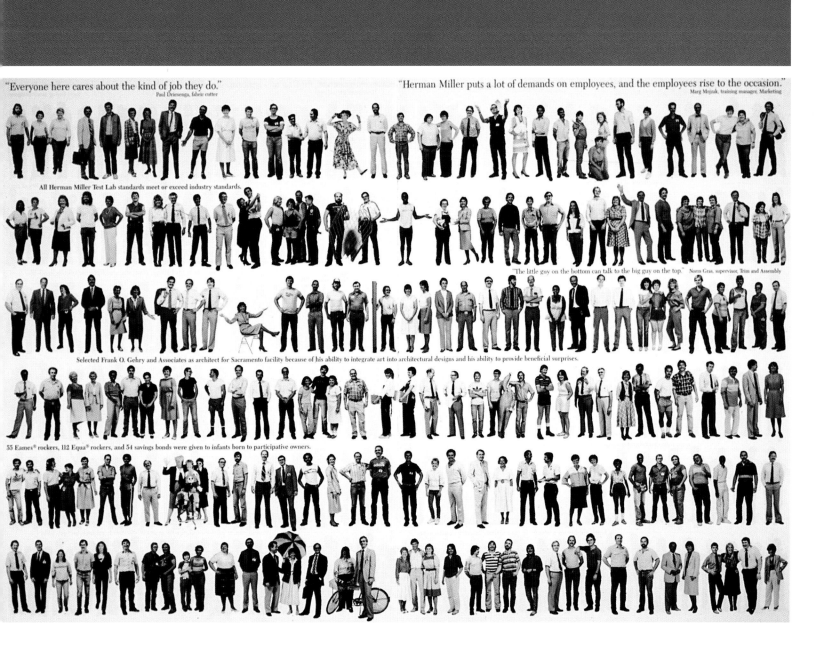

"Everyone here cares about the kind of job they do."
Paul Driesenga, fabric cutter

"Herman Miller puts a lot of demands on employees, and the employees rise to the occasion."
Marg Mojzak, training manager, Marketing

All Herman Miller Test Lab standards meet or exceed industry standards.

"The little guy on the bottom can talk to the big guy on the top." Norm Gras, supervisor, Trim and Assembly

Selected Frank O. Gehry and Associates as architect for Sacramento facility because of his ability to integrate art into architectural designs and his ability to provide beneficial surprises.

55 Eames® rockers, 112 Equa® rockers, and 34 savings bonds were given to infants born to participative owners.

VISUAL COMMUNICATIONS TO REFLECT THE SPIRIT OF A COMPANY

WE BELIEVE THE TRUTH IS GOOD ENOUGH.

The business importance of quality graphics had been established early at Herman Miller by George Nelson, who created the first corporate identity program. His designs for logos and sales catalogs communicated the principles of quality, honesty, and good design (see chapter 2). Soon after, Charles and Ray Eames contributed their graphic talents to Herman Miller's packaging, advertisements, and product literature, and a series of talented graphic designers followed.

The company's printed materials have two major goals: to communicate information clearly and usefully and to reflect the creative nature of its enterprise. The firm's philosophy that open information is as critical to success as the quality and design of a product pertains to communications with all of the company constituents: employees, dealers, architects and designers, clients, and the community. Max De Pree, son of the founder, former CEO, and chairman was fond of saying, "Err on the side of over-communicating."

When the company went public in 1970, the Eames Office designed the stock certificate. They embellished its center with a bouquet of wildflowers native to West Michigan.

For their first formal annual report, Herman Miller turned to graphic designer consultant John Massey, well known for his graphic design work for the Container Corporation.

Herman Miller wanted to provide the required SEC information in a manner that reflected the spirit of the company. Massey designed a beautiful screened poster with the financial reports set off in perforated tear-off sections, so that the shareholder, after reviewing the figures, could remove them and be left with a work of art worthy of display. Massey's surprising financial poster set the tone for future reports. His 1974 report, to accommodate a reduced budget, was printed on newsprint with content primarily taken from the company's staff newsletters.

In 1976, Steve Frykholm was put in charge of creating the annual reports. A graduate of Cranbrook Academy of Art (the alma mater of Charles and Ray Eames), he had joined Herman Miller six years earlier and began providing his talents to corporate graphics. He was responsible for brochures, stationery, price books, internal newsletters, the graphics on company trucks, and posters for the company's annual picnic. Herman Miller's graphic and communication materials have been widely honored. The

herman miller president's report 1970

Highlights

Change continues to be a dominating reality

Major increases in orders, shipments, and income
Our business clearly defined and direction set
Educational centers opened
New systems and products designed
Manufacturing space doubled
International organization expanded
International design program started

Financial

Herman Miller today

Change is the dominating reality

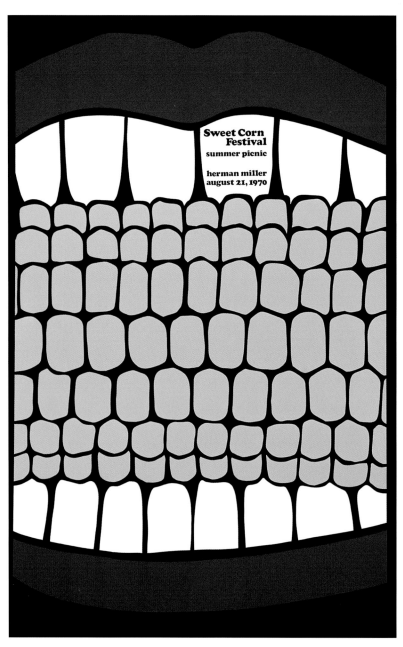

The tradition of a Herman Miller picnic started early in the life of the company. D.J. De Pree and his wife, Nellie, initially provided home-cooked food for all employees in their backyard or a local park. As the company grew so did picnic logistics as well as the creation of posters used to communicate the date. In 2003 6,300 people registered for the picnic. Steve Frykholm designed the first poster in 1970 and did his last one in 1989. They were looked forward to by employees and became coveted pieces of art. The posters are now sold by the Museum of Modern Art and constitute a collection that has been ongoing for over thirty years.

herman miller summer picnic   july 28, 1984

"As an owner, you approach your job in a different way, a more responsive way."
Richard Bennett, program manager, New Technology

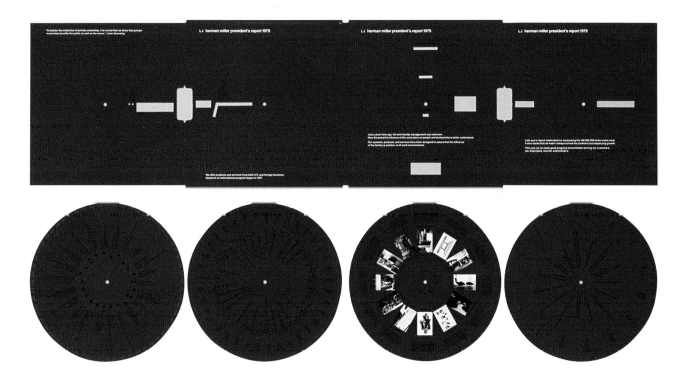

American Institute of Graphic Arts (AIGA) has granted them both their gold medal and twenty-five-year awards. Frykholm's picnic posters became collectibles and are now included in the permanent collections of art museums throughout the world.

Frykholm believes that annual reports should be "more than a moment in time"; pointing out that the financial results are already history when they're published. The report should help the company build a relationship with interested constituents, stockholders, customers, employees, architects, and designers—and, of course, satisfy Wall Street.

At one time there was a rigid Herman Miller corporate identity manual that proved to be restrictive rather than supportive. Although well intended, such a strict manual can be unnecessarily rigid and inhibit the creation of the most appropriate communication solution.

Today, there are guidelines and the recognition that the designed solution should fit the communication need, not a manual. Consistency can help reinforce a particular message, but it is also useful to remember Emerson's quote, "Consistency is the hobgoblin of little minds."

Frykholm's annual reports ignore a consistent format, and are packed with visual surprise. They've ranged from small booklets to a *volvelle* (information wheel), a brochure with balloons and confetti attached, and a large one-page document with a series of intricate folds.

The annual report of 1985 celebrated the year when all employees became shareholders. Frykholm decided to include a picture of every employee in the report. At that time Herman Miller had more than 3,300 employees spread over several states and foreign countries. He assigned a team of photographers and assistants to set up a common background and photograph every employee. It was an ambitious project, and it made for a strong annual report—one that several other companies have imitated.

In 1994, a paper entitled "Communications at Herman Miller" was developed to codify how communication materials should be developed among the many parts of the organization.

The opening paragraph states:

PROBLEMS   SOLVED

Herman Miller graphics reinforced the company brand not by rigid consistent use of typography but more by consistent concern for clear communication to the multiple audiences served. The use of the logo and ligature has gone through several of its own iterations and adaptations to new technologies.

We believe the truth is good enough. Communicating the truth requires hard work and vigilance. Because Herman Miller and the industry are complex, we know that our efforts to communicate the truth are sometimes not good enough. Just as we try to design products that bring clarity and richness to the work environments, we try to design communication that brings clarity and richness to what we have to say. To that end: We try to make every communication simple, recognizing how much the complexity of the message can vary. We try to avoid the pretentious and the simplistic. We know that our audience is at times a single entity but is more often made up of several discrete groups. Some messages are essentially verbal but require illustration. Some messages are primarily visual but need words to complement what is shown. We use communications media as skillfully and responsibly as we can, trying to make certain that the subject fits the medium. Communications is not an end in itself but part of a process that involves the customer and is aimed at continued learning and understanding.

Although the audiences for any company's communications vary, Herman Miller identified its key constituents as architects, designers, customers, investors, employees, and the community. The company has stated, "We communicate to our customers and end users of our products through face-to-face communications supported by

product literature and research information that helps recognize how a product can help meet their needs. Our communications to people who influence our customers help explain how to understand, plan, order, and manage our product. While visually compatible in some instances, these materials vary in their presentation depending on the product line, a sign that each of our products has its own integrity. We try to provide information, not only for the application of the product, but also an understanding of its concept, development, and use in the workplace."

All corporate graphic design aims to align words, imagery, and typography to convey the actions taken by the company and the policies behind them. To help ensure consistency and recognizing the role of technology, the Herman Miller company developed principles on information and communications:

Renewal has been a constant at Herman Miller for the last 50 years. Beginning as a manufacturer of imitative but high-quality residential furniture, Herman Miller evolved into an innovative organization that has had a

significant impact on the industry.   Our recent rapid growth and expansion are due primarily to our systems, the first of which was the Action Office® system introduced

in earlier products, like George Nelson's Comprehensive Storage System, or Charles Eames's Contract Storage Units, or even the Executive Office Group designed

invented by Robert L. Propst, brought these seeds to fruition. With this came a new, more aggressive management stance. These new concepts in furnishing the work

and we evolved from an item company to a systems company, renewing an entire industry in the process. The Action Office system was the first open-pla

fastest-growing segment of the furniture industry.   From a focus on individual product solutions, we moved to a focus on customer need in relation to the entire work process in offices, laboratories, health-care

facilities, light-assembly plants, and related work environments. This opened the door to multiple applications of the systems concepts, expressed through Co/Struc,® Action Factory,® and Action Laboratory.® We discovered

through this research the trend toward the blurring of the sharp demarcation between kinds of work: Much work done in offices, such as the processing of insurance claims, is becoming more and more like work done in

manufacturing facilities. Work done in places where electronics or similar products are assembled has become more like office work.   Study of the work process also broadened our view of "product" to include information

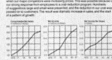

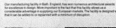

and services. The customer is buying a result, not just hardware, and knowledge is part of the creating of that result.   Within Herman Miller, openness to change has led to a different kind of innovation, through participatory

management. Our history with the Scanlon process began in 1950, when Dr. Carl Frost began working with Herman Miller management to introduce the principles of cooperative labor relations. The plan was re-designed

in 1979, maintaining the principles on which the plan is based but updating the structure.   The Herman Miller that the outside world sees is really a manifestation of a climate of renewal.

1991 Annual Report   Herman Miller, Inc. and Subsidiaries

Renewal has been a constant at Herman Miller for the last 50 years. Beginning as a manufacturer of imitative but high-quality residential furniture, Herman Miller evolved into an innovative organization that has had a significant impact on the industry.

Our recent rapid growth and expansion are due primarily to our systems, the first of which was the Action Office® system introduced in 1968. But the seeds of the systems concept were present in earlier products, like George Nelson's Comprehensive Storage System, or Charles Eames's Contract Storage Units, or even the Executive Office Group designed by Gilbert Rohde in the 1930s.

The Action Office system, invented by Robert L. Propst, brought these seeds to fruition. With this came a new, more aggressive management stance. These new concepts in furnishing the workplace coincided with a strengthening of sales and marketing, and we evolved from an item company to a systems company, renewing an entire industry in the process. The Action Office system was the first open-plan system marketed in the U.S., and open-plan is now the fastest-growing segment of the furniture industry.

From a focus on individual product solutions, we moved to a focus on customer need in relation to the entire work process in offices, laboratories, health-care facilities, light-assembly plants, and related work environments. This opened the door to multiple applications of the systems concepts, expressed through Co/Struc,® Action Factory,® and Action Laboratory.® We discovered through this research the trend toward the blurring of the sharp demarcation between kinds of work: Much work done in offices, such as the processing of insurance claims, is becoming more and more like work done in manufacturing facilities. Work done in places where electronics or similar products are assembled has become more like office work.

Study of the work process also broadened our view of "product" to include information and services. The customer is buying a result, not just hardware, and knowledge is part of the creating of that result.

herman miller

Information

* Information belongs to everybody, it is no one group's property
* Free access to information is as critical to our success as the quality and design of a product
* Every worker is a knowledge worker
* Every employee is the most competent judge of what information he/she can use
* Information is to be questioned, refined, and supplemented—not simply presented
* We cannot be adaptive or relational—or even survive—without open and abundant information

Communication

* The way we communicate expresses our beliefs about people
* Communicating always invites people in to develop more meaning. When two people truly communicate, each person learns something
* There is a person behind every communication
* Everyone at Herman Miller is obliged to speak out and listen
* We structure information to account for various ways of thinking and perceiving
* We actively seek new, diverse, rich, complex, contradictory, overlapping sources of information
* Communication is an expression of our similarities/dissimilarities and agreements/dis-agreements

Herman Miller, from George Nelson's first product catalogs to today's Web sites, works continually to hone their corporate identity. Good communications are possible only when they align with the words that are spoken or presented, the actions that are taken, and the company policies that support the organization. Such alignment is not always easy to achieve, but ignoring it can result in poor communications or just plain hype. Herman Miller takes the challenge seriously, and achieves a closer alignment of words, actions, and policies than do most companies.

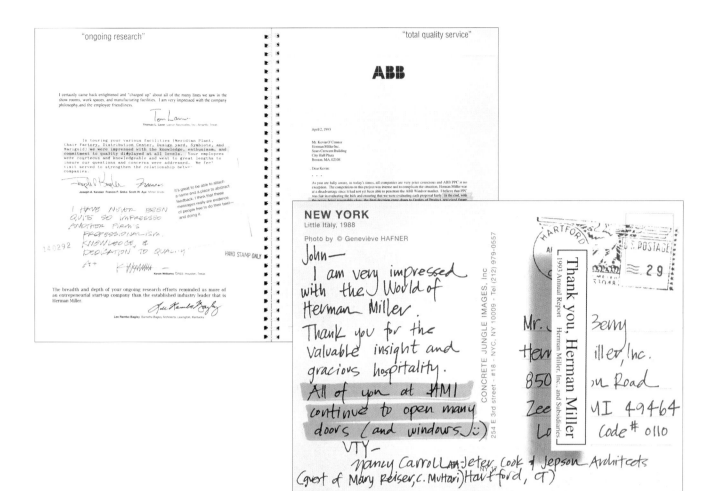

"ongoing research"

"total quality service"

I certainly came back enlightened and "charged up" about all of the many lines we saw in the show rooms, work spaces, and manufacturing facilities. I am very impressed with the company philosophy and the employee friendliness.

Thomas L. Leon, Leon Associates, Inc., Amarillo, Texas

In touring your various facilities (Meridian Plant, Chair Factory, Distribution Center, Design yard, Symbiote, and Marigold) we were impressed with the knowledge, enthusiasm, and commitment to quality displayed at all levels. Your employees were courteous and knowledgeable and went to great lengths to insure our questions and concerns were addressed. We feel visit served to strengthen the relationship between companies.

Joseph A. Kessler, Frances P. Setka, Scott W. Ayo, Miller Blum

I HAVE NEVER BEEN QUITE SO IMPRESSED ANOTHER FIRM'S PROFESSIONALISM, KNOWLEDGE, & DEDICATION TO QUALITY.

140292

A+

Kevin Williams, ERGS, Houston, Texas

HAND STAMP ONLY

It's great to be able to attach a name and a place to abstract feedback. I think that these messages really are evidence of people free to do their best—and doing it.

The breadth and depth of your ongoing research efforts reminded us more of an entrepreneurial start-up company than the established industry leader that is Herman Miller.

Lee Rambo Bagley, Barretta Bagley Architects, Lexington, Kentucky

ABB

April 2, 1993

Mr. Kevin O'Connor
Herman Miller Inc.
Sears-Crescent Building
City Hall Plaza
Boston, MA. 02108

Dear Kevin:

. . .

As you are fully aware, in today's times, all companies are very price conscious and ABB PPC is no exception. The competition on this project was intense and to complicate the situation, Herman Miller was at a disadvantage since it had not yet been able to penetrate the ABB Windsor market. I believe that PPC was fair in evaluating the bids and ensuring that we were evaluating each proposal fairly. In the end, with the prices being reasonably close, the final decision came down to Quality of Product, perceived future...

NEW YORK
Little Italy, 1988
Photo by © Geneviève HAFNER

CONCRETE JUNGLE IMAGES, Inc
254 E 3rd street - #18 - NYC, NY 10009 - Tel (212) 979-0557

John—
I am very impressed with the World of Herman Miller.
Thank you for the valuable insight and gracious hospitality.
All of you at AMI continue to open many doors (and windows. :)
VTY—
Nancy Carroll AIA-Jeter Cook & Jepson Architects
(guest of Mary Reiser, C. Muttari) Hartford, CT)

HARTFORD

U.S. POSTAGE ≡ .29

Thank you, Herman Miller
1993 Annual Report
Herman Miller, Inc. and Subsidiaries

Mr. J...
Herm...
850...
Zee...
Lo...

Berry
iller, Inc.
n Road
MI 49464
Code # 0110

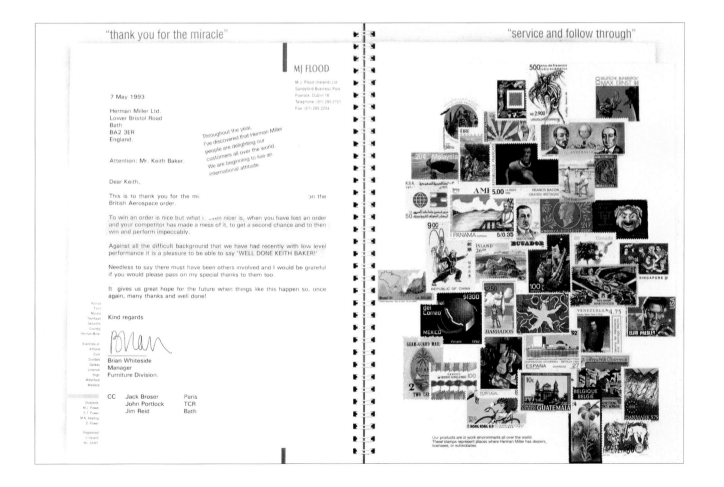

"thank you for the miracle"

"service and follow through"

MJ FLOOD

M.J. Flood (Ireland) Ltd
Sandyford Business Park
Foxrock, Dublin 18
Telephone (01) 295 2701
Fax (01) 295 2254

7 May 1993

Herman Miller Ltd.
Lower Bristol Road
Bath
BA2 3ER
England.

Attention: Mr. Keith Baker.

Dear Keith,

Throughout the year, I've discovered that Herman Miller people are delighting our customers all over the world. We are beginning to live an international attitude.

This is to thank you for the mi... on the British Aerospace order.

To win an order is nice but what i ...even nicer is, when you have lost an order and your competitor has made a mess of it, to get a second chance and to then win and perform impeccably.

Against all the difficult background that we have had recently with low level performance it is a pleasure to be able to say 'WELL DONE KEITH BAKER!'

Needless to say there must have been others involved and I would be grateful if you would please pass on my special thanks to them too.

It gives us great hope for the future when things like this happen so, once again, many thanks and well done!

Kind regards

Brian Whiteside
Manager
Furniture Division.

CC   Jack Broser   Paris
      John Portlock   TCR
      Jim Reid   Bath

Our products are in work environments all over the world. These stamps represent places where Herman Miller has dealers, licensees, or subsidiaries.

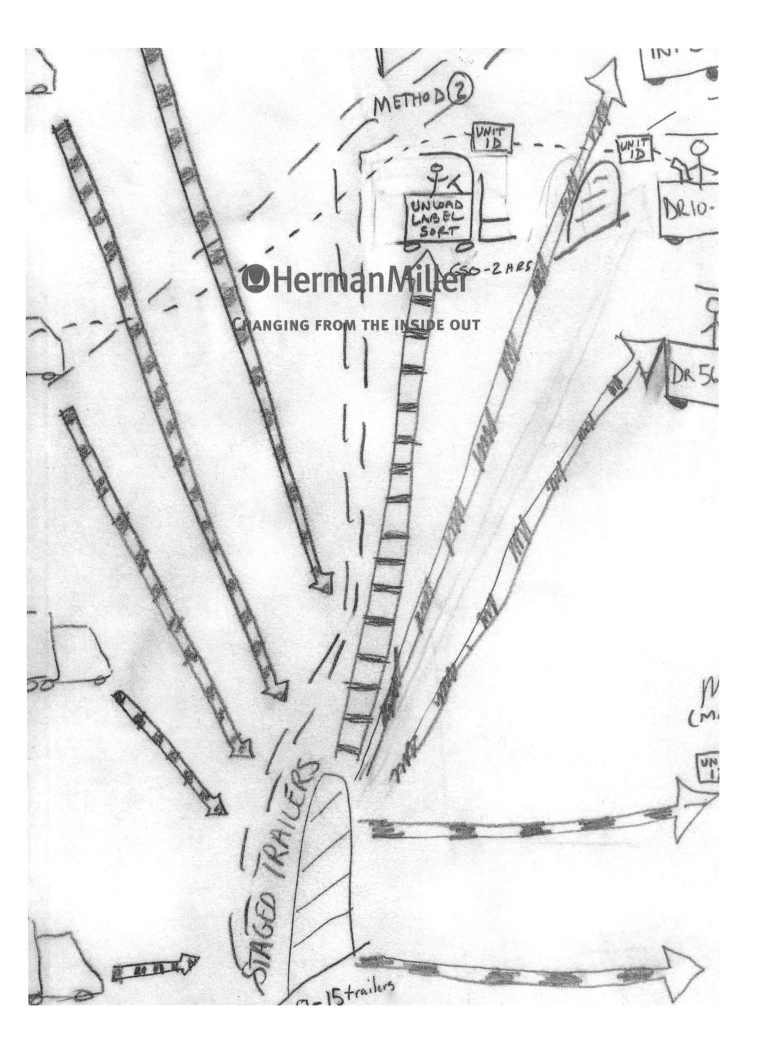

1994 Annual Report   Herman Miller, Inc., and Subsidiaries

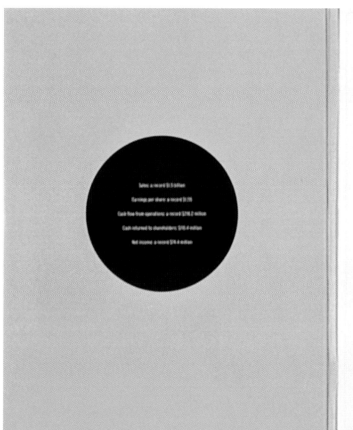

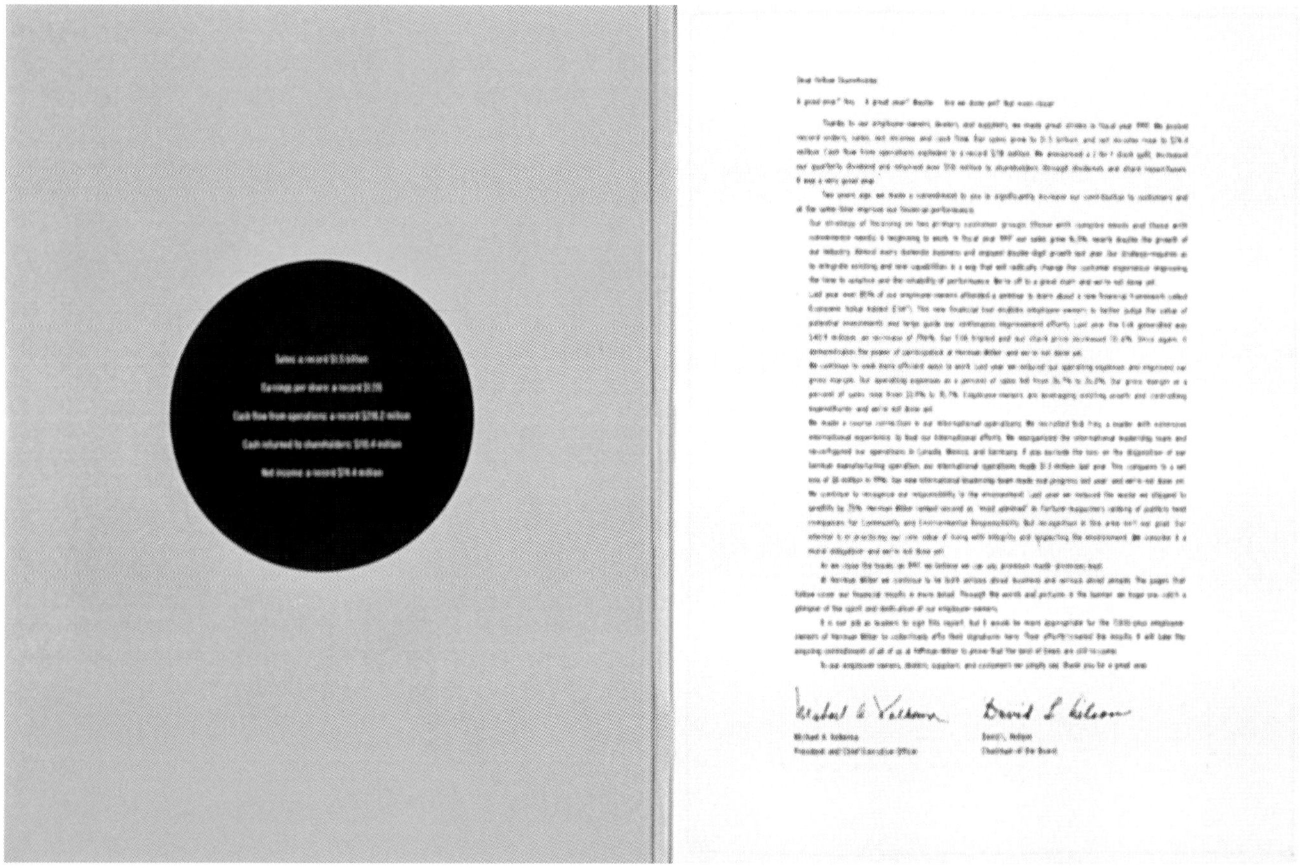

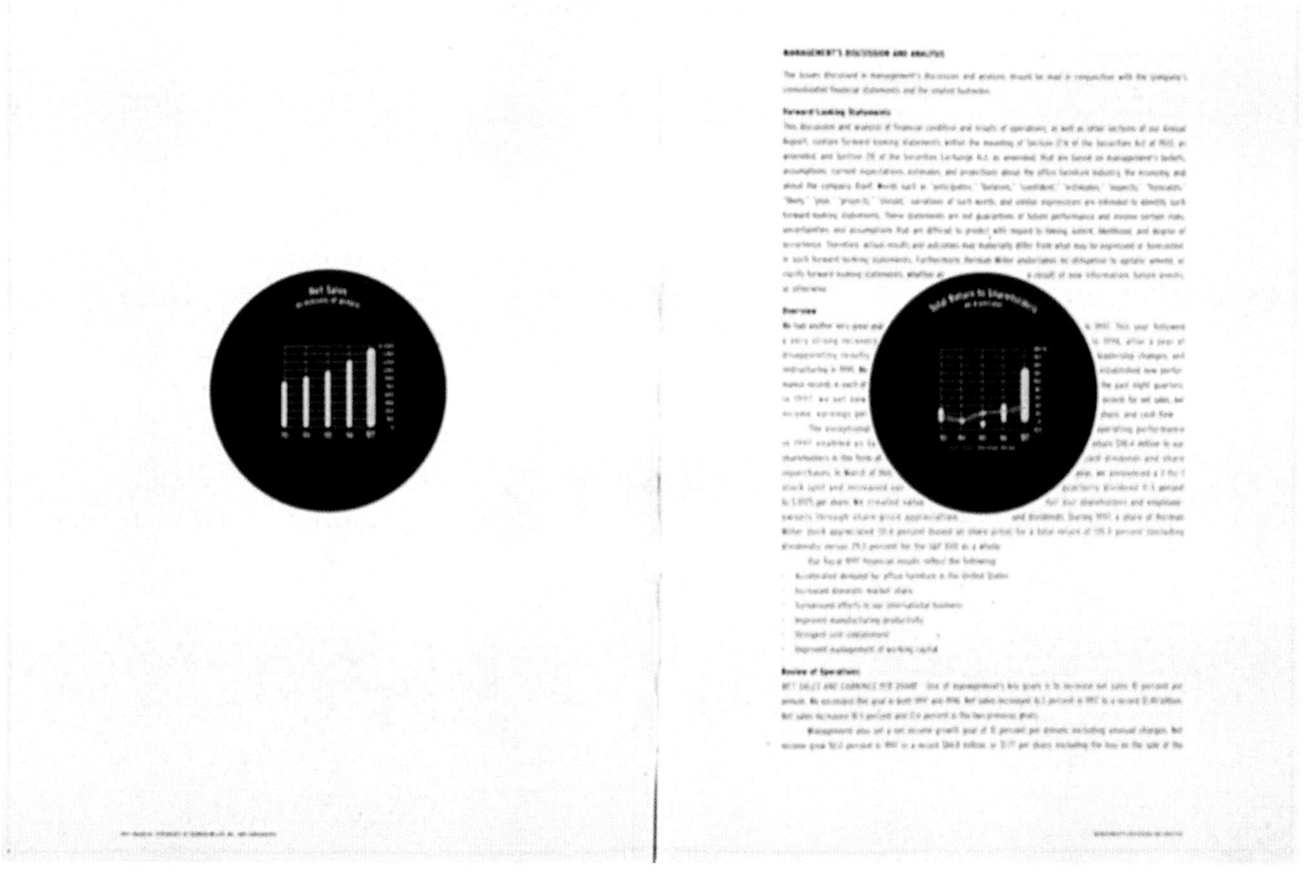

Sales a record $1.5 billion

Earnings per share a record $1.59

Cash flow from operations a record $176.2 million

Cash returned to shareholders $176.4 million

Net income a record $74.4 million

Dear Fellow Shareholder:

A good one? Yes. A great one? Maybe — Are we done yet? No, not even close.

Michael A. Volkema
President and Chief Executive Officer

David L. Nelson
Chairman of the Board

MANAGEMENT'S DISCUSSION AND ANALYSIS

The issues discussed in management's discussion and analysis should be read in conjunction with the company's consolidated financial statements and the related footnotes.

Forward-Looking Statements

(text largely illegible)

Overview

(text largely illegible)

Review of Operations

(text largely illegible)

ETHOSPACE® SYSTEM

The world's premier frame-and-tile system, Ethospace offers practically unlimited aesthetic and functional possibilities.

As Herman Miller's m of perform

CHAPTER 8 : **FACILITY MANAGEMENT**
F.M.I.

Research Report

The
Departm...
Social
Offi...
In...

The
Senator Hat...
Office Inno...
Project

A report on the inf...
responsive enviro...
on satisfaction a...

Facility Influence
on Productivity

A report on the influence of a responsive
environment on satisfaction and
proficiency in an educational setting

...arch project integrating an
...e educational program with an
...al setting at Michigan State
...sing, Michigan.

The office
A facility based
on change

By Robert Propst

A NEW PROFESSION TO MANAGE THE NEW OFFICE SYSTEMS

"FROM THE PEOPLE WHO BROUGHT YOU THE PROBLEM, HERE'S THE SOLUTION..."

In the 1970s, less than ten years after its introduction, Herman Miller realized that the flexibility inherent in its open office system, Action Office, was not being fully utilized. The quality of an open office workspace was being compromised, and the capability to individualize a space was often neglected. Although it was designed to adjust to changing office needs easily, in most organizations, the flexible system became, in practice, fixed, primarily because no one was explicitly responsible for such changes. Architects and interior designers specified the products, but once the system was installed, they were not called on to make the changes. Human-resource departments did not have the experience nor expertise to make physical changes. Maintenance personnel fixed minor problems, but were not assigned the reconfiguration of office systems. And few companies saw the usage of their facility as an asset to manage. A new type of professional responsibility was needed; to fulfill that need Herman Miller established the Facility Management Institute (FMI) in Ann Arbor, Michigan. (Within Herman Miller, some wry observers suggested the slogan, "From the people who brought you the problem, here's the solution.")

The company's "need" statement for the establishment of the FMI read, "Facility management is an emerging new management science that must be a continuing function in any modern organization. In order for the work environment to meet ongoing requirements, management must learn the skills of integrating facilities and the work process, coping with change, growth, and improvement; and they must assume the responsibility for the necessary decision making. The progressive organization will incorporate facility management as one of its important prerogatives." It involved a full understanding of the physical plant of a business, including issues of management, finance, construction, real estate, or managing industrial suppliers. The FMI created courses and programs including:

* Financial management of facility properties
* Building acquisition—principles and guidelines
* Testing measurement of facility effectiveness
* Aesthetics of interior architecture
* Human factors and facility effectiveness

The Facility Management Institute was meant, primarily, to raise corporate awareness of facility management as a legitimate function in corporate decision making. However, related responsibilities were also acknowledged, from educating corporate personnel about facility decisions, to establishing a science and knowledge center of integrated facility management, and delineating the principles and practices that would form the basis of this new discipline. Herman Miller also recognized the need to establish a professional association to foster the professionalism of facility management.

It is an unusual enterprise to create an entirely new profession, and questions arose about how the task should be defined. How does one know when a profession has been established? Due to a lack of existing criteria, Herman Miller created its own framework. They determined that a profession had been established when there were a number of colleges and universities teaching a class on Facilities Management, when a portion of Fortune 500 companies had "facility manager" positions, a professional association with at least 1,000 members, and a trade publication serving the field.

In 1985 these criteria were met, and Herman Miller realized that for the profession of Facility Management to grow, it could no longer be seen as an offshoot of the company. The professional association, IFMA (International Facility Management Association), had been founded in 1980 and housed in the FMI building in Michigan. It was moved to Dallas, Texas, where it has continued to grow steadily. The FMI in Ann Arbor was closed, and the research projects under way at that time were incorporated into Herman Miller's Design and Development.

Today, the field of facility management is thriving. After declining slightly in the late 1990s and early 2000s when much of it was outsourced, it has made a comeback by allying itself even more strongly with architects and interior designers. Although many office workers are not aware of its presence, building owners, lease agents, and human-resources departments are keenly aware of the special skills of facility managers.

The Facilities Management Institute was primarily an educational organization. The building designed and constructed in Ann Arbor, Michigan was to meet the educational needs of the instructional programs FMI created. While some primary research was accomplished in the facility the majority of research was done in other locations. The access to talented individuals at the University of Michigan was beneficial to the intention of FMI and helpful on specific research efforts like the MetaForm project.

CHAPTER 9 : **METAFORM**
UNIVERSAL DESIGN

NEW TOOLS FOR INDEPENDENT LIVING

DESIGNERS STUDIED ACTIVITIES AS DIVERSE AS TRANS-
PORTING GROCERIES FROM THE CAR TO THE KITCHEN,
SLEEPING, ENTERTAINING, AND PERSONAL HYGIENE.

Research investigations of the issues and
needs for long-term seating for an aging
population

In 1986 and 1987 the Herman Miller Research Corporation turned to the subject
of aging. They set about discovering the tools that would allow aging people to
live independently longer. They consulted with a wide range of experts, including
a former Secretary of Health, Education, and Welfare; an industrial designer; a
gerontologist; a bio-statistician; a physician; and a group of appropriately aged
individuals. The answers—large and complex—led to the MetaForm project.

Six designers were selected to work on specific elements identified through
the research, from long-term sitting to personal hygiene, sleeping, food preparation, and labor efficiency (such as how to move groceries from car to refrigerator
and cupboard, or how to move dishes from table to dishwasher to cupboard).
Four goals were established for the various products under development. They
had to respond to genuine needs of older or disabled people; appeal to any pro-
gressively minded person regardless of age; be designed primarily for use in the
home but also for use in other environments such as nursing homes; and they
must not stigmatize their users as old or disabled.

As part of the company's Research Corporation facility in Ann Arbor, a Living Arts Studio was created. It included both full-scale and scale-modeled residential environments that covered all aspects of independent living. Designers studied activities as diverse as transporting groceries from the car to the kitchen, sleeping, entertaining, and personal hygiene. Concepts were developed, modeled, prototyped, and tested. At various stages of development, focus groups were invited in to test the products.

No detail went unexamined. Designer Gian Zaccai developed a range of fixtures for personal hygiene, such as toilets, bathtubs, and showers and prototyped the designs in full scale. Bill Stumpf and Don Chadwick created several seating options for long-term comfort and greatly enhanced their understanding of that specialty. On a smaller scale, a complete kitchen—down to the faucets, refrigerator, and cooking capabilities—was designed for use by the elderly. Other initiatives included a bed, textiles, tables, lamps, color schemes, and a conveyer belt that would move food from the refrigerator to the stove.

Despite the enormous hard work, the clear mission, and the high financial investment, however, the MetaForm Project was eventually put on hold because a distribution system did not exist. There was no existing way for Herman Miller to sell the products to the intended customers. Stores specializing in home products for the aging were not set up to sell full environments, and they were often uninviting commercial spaces. Herman Miller realized that to be successful in this effort, they would need to create an entirely new distribution system, new manufacturing processes, and create and educate a new sales and support structure. These undertakings would have made the products prohibitively expensive.

Much of the research that had already been completed, in particular Stumpf and Chadwick's study of long-term sitting, went into other products. They applied their MetaForm lessons of flexibility, variable heights, and prevention of heat build-up into the now ubiquitous Aeron chair that is coveted by people of all ages (see chapter 12).

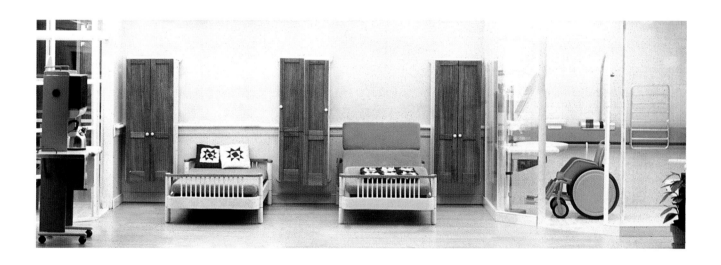

The full range of residential needs was studied with the MetaForm Project. Parking, moving food items from a garage to a kitchen, sleeping and typical living room uses were all taken into consideration and prototyped in scale models.

The Sarah chair was researched and developed to provide a location where the aging population can have a place that accommodates the various activities one might have during the day—reading, eating, writing, working, crafts work—while accommodating the physical needs of being able to recline, get out of the chair and be supported.

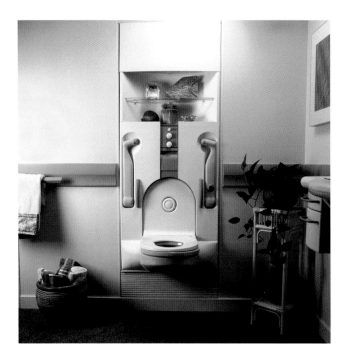

Full-scale mock-ups of a bathroom facility incorporate the principles of universal design. The toilet node is not merely a fixture but an appliance that adjusts itself to conform to the needs of each individual user. To accommodate all users, the distance heights can range from 24" to 10.5" from the floor, for a small child to a tall adult or a disabled elder. The armrests can be used optionally and can facilitate safe transfers from a wheelchair to the seat.

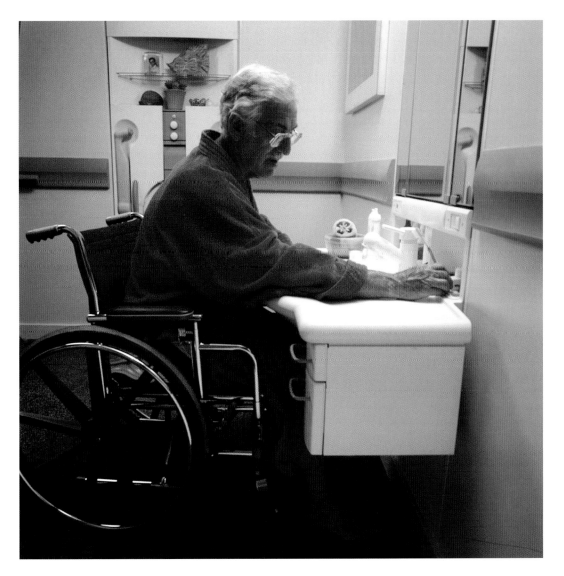

The sink node part of the MetaForm Project was designed to be adjusted vertically from a height of 24" to 42", from the top of the sink to the floor. This range accommodates the needs of either standing or seated users of all sizes. Wheelchair users have unimpeded knee access and can use the clear space under the sink for the necessary turn radius.

RECYCLE, REFURBISH, REDESIGN
TO SERVE A NEW MARKET

MILLER SQA BECAME A FULLY DEVELOPED SUBSIDIARY,
WITH ITS OWN FACILITY, GRAPHICS, AND ORDERING SYSTEM.

In the mid-1980s, the Action Office modular system (see chapter 5) had been in production for more than twenty years. It was installed in numerous offices, and as businesses changed, offices were remodeled and new modular systems were purchased. Although they were of high quality, with good materials, the used Action Office systems were being discarded. With an ongoing concern for the environment, Herman Miller instituted a program to take back products for refurbishment. The program, initially called Tradex, reduced materials going to landfills by allowing trade-ins when buying new systems furniture.

Around the same time, there was a boom in small and mid-sized businesses. Action Office had been conceived with large corporations in mind—companies with generous budgets, spacious offices, and specialized planners available to

PREVIOUS SPREAD

1997 Promotional photo of Equa chairs and Q-system

→ **1998** Folder cover used for multiple purposes, depicting the character of the organization

↓ **circa 1996** P-system with Avian chairs

Simple, Quick & Affordable office furniture

Miller SQA. Inc.   10201 Adams Street   Holland. MI 49424-9168   800 253 2733   616 772 4129 fax   www.sqa.net

help tailor the system to a company's specific needs. These new smaller companies, however, with their relatively tight budgets, created a new market for refurbished products and simpler office systems. Demand outpaced Herman Miller's inventory of used products, so they began to design new office systems with a reduced number of components and options.

Along with the product itself, this new market required a simplified distribution system. Herman Miller's network of dealerships was designed to serve large complex customers. Diverse components were required, involving sophisticated multiple manufacturing sites, and had complex ordering and fulfillment systems. Action Office alone provided literally thousands of combinations for multiple options. A new office system with limited components and options—as few as five choices—streamlined specifying, ordering, and receiving products. The new system was called Miller SQA, for "simple, quick, and affordable."

Miller SQA became a fully developed subsidiary, with its own facility, graphics, and ordering system. Without specialized space planners on staff, small businesses needed

↑ SQA headquarters and manufacturing
facility designed by Bill McDonough

OVERLEAF

1998 Q System—a Best of Neocon Gold
Design Award Winner

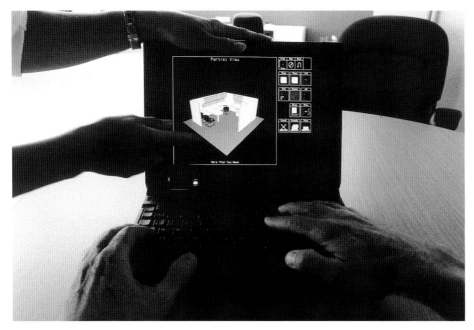

Industry's first software developed for use
with customers to select, visualize, price,
and order office system products

an easy planning and ordering system, and Miller SQA's answer was Z-Net, the first
electronic visualization, planning, and ordering process in the furniture industry.

Although it might appear that Miller SQA would compete with Herman Miller's original dealerships, the products and services offered by both were well differentiated.
Indeed, when Miller SQA was launched, sales increased for all parts of Herman Miller.
An internal review of SQA published in 1998 stated, "It has created a new way of selling
office furniture and learned to serve the 'convenience' customers it identified. It has also
created a new way of managing the whole business as an integrated system from raw
materials vendors to ultimate users."

Growing at a 35% annual rate, Miller SQA's success prompted the management of
Herman Miller to emulate its model in all operations. In the early 2000s, the Miller SQA
subsidiary was merged into the larger company, and rapid maneuverability became
Herman Miller's new focus.

It means what you see is what you get.

Great office furniture without getting soaked.

It means two-day quick ship.

Series of images used to build awareness
for ads, brochures and billboards

1998 Q System with Equa chairs

CHAPTER 11 : **THE DESIGN YARD**

[RECOGNIZED NEED]
A BUILDING FOR RESEARCH, DESIGN, AND DEVELOPMENT

"FARMS ARE ABOUT NURTURING AND GROWING, AND SO IS THE DESIGN PROCESS."

In the 1980s, Herman Miller decided to build one centralized facility to support the design process. A 1986 design brief explained that consolidating to one site wasn't only important—it was essential:

> Design at Herman Miller, beginning with an idea, is sustained with spiritual concern and technical expertise. The ability of the often fragile and vulnerable design idea to mature requires extraordinary personal commitment from both the designer and the Herman Miller support staff. Integral with this commitment is the expressed need to nurture, critique, evaluate, model and test a design. The process is reiterative by nature, and yet it currently suffers from being dispersed throughout a number of locations. Coming together in one location will create the opportunity to release and focus the energies of the team members in a communal way as yet unknown to Herman Miller.

A site was chosen in Holland, Michigan, and the Minneapolis-based architecture firm of Meyer, Scherer & Rockcastle was selected for the project. Jeff Scherer became the lead designer.

The architects took into consideration the following requirements of the occupant. Each design team would have its own private studio, and all the studios would have easy access to the facilities for model-making, engineering, testing, and experimental manufacturing. The space should encourage casual interactions. The design legacies of Charles Eames and George Nelson would be carried out in spaces that provided inspiration, used materials honestly, and gave

PREVIOUS SPREAD

LEFT: **2000** Design yard meeting room near reception area

RIGHT: **1989** Design yard

→ **1989** Porch entrance to a research area

visitors at least one new idea. As the program developed, Scherer began to consider the metaphor of a farm.

"We liked the way farms are set up with several related outbuildings," said Scherer. "Each building has a separate function, yet all are necessary to the overall working of the farm. The design process (at Herman Miller) works very much the same way. Each group needs enough separation to work without distractions, yet they all need proximity to the other groups to foster the kind of creative give-and-take that really develops ideas."

"Besides," Scherer added, "farms are about nurturing and growing, and so is the design process. The only difference is that these people nurture and grow ideas."

The award-winning campus, dubbed the "Design Yard," indeed resembles a farm. The "barns" are design studios, the silos are conference rooms, entryways became front porches, and corridors are covered walkways. A booklet prepared for the facility's dedication describes the project: "The Design Yard brings together the old and the new, the rural and the urban, the surprising and the familiar, and the minds and disciplines essential for product development. Through the careful merging of these things comes a curi-

→ **2000** Coffee Bar-Bombo series stools by Magis of Italy near the entrance to provide purposeful space for unexpected interactions

↓ **2000** "Backyard" area behind Leadership Team workstations— it provides space and support for team activities

ous union. A farm becomes a logical setting for the design and development of products; a combination of shapes, materials, and highly advanced work is completely at home among cows and a village and a growing city. Spaces to work privately and communally give minds and disciplines a creative and productive environment in which to dream and build and plan."

In 2000, the Design Yard was reconfigured to include the corporate headquarters. Senior executives moved to gain from the benefits the environment provided and be closer to the design and development area. Their offices, which are small, open into shared common areas called "backyards," and are furnished with casual residential-style furniture—comfortable surroundings for what can be high-energy discussions. The proximity of executive decision-making and the design and development process significantly speeds up the time needed to move an idea into reality.

The Design Yard also encourages casual interaction. A café in the entry area pro-

PREVIOUS SPREAD

1987 Design yard cafeteria for meals and gatherings of large groups

↓ **1992** Engineering department entrance at design yard with silo conference room

CLOCKWISE FROM TOP LEFT

2000 Executive leadership office space

2000 Executive backyard library and casual interaction meeting area

1987 Coffee bar area with retired Eames fiberglass mold converted to a frog sculpture

2000 Front door reception with water fountain

OVERLEAF

2000 Executive leadership backyard space for casual interaction among senior management and guests

vides plenty of comfortable seating and refreshments. But these seemingly casual environs increase the likelihood of conversation, engagement—the sharing of ideas that bring to mind principles first evidenced about a good working environment in Robert Propst's *The Office: A Facility Based on Change.* Propst, who in 1960 proclaimed "today's office is a wasteland. It saps vitality, blocks talent, frustrates accomplishment. It is the daily scene of unfulfilled intentions and failed effort," sought to improve the conditions within the office, believing that a better office equals greater productivity and more inspired work results. From that problem recognition came Herman Miller's continued focus on research of the changing needs in knowledge work.

The Design Yard embodies Herman Miller's belief that information should flow horizontally not up and down an organization. The result is a non-intimidating, relaxed environment. The combination of sophistication and folk art humor reflects the character of the company and draws upon its cultural past. Herman Miller is indeed practicing what it preaches.

⬆ **2000** Parlor for meetings and information sharing

➡ **2000** Hallway between main areas with marshmallow sofa and ebony Eames molded plywood screen

OVERLEAF

1986 Design yard

CHAPTER 12 : AERON
BILL STUMPF AND DON CHADWICK

THE WORLD'S MOST COMFORTABLE OFFICE CHAIR

AT EVEN THE EARLIEST STAGES, IT BECAME CLEAR THAT THE RESULTING CHAIR WAS GOING TO LOOK RADICALLY DIFFERENT FROM ALL PREVIOUS MODELS.

During the MetaForm research project (see chapter 9), Bill Stumpf and Don Chadwick discovered that comfortable long-term sitting required flexibility, variable heights, and the reduction of heat build-up. Their investigation revealed that no mechanism existed to ease the transition from reclining to standing. As MetaForm was disbanded, they recognized that these same seating needs also applied to the workplace. Stumpf and Chadwick proposed a work chair to satisfy these problems. Thus began the development of what would become the Aeron chair.

From the goals identified in the Metaform project, they added their beliefs that:

* Ergonomically, the chair should actively promote the health of the person who sits in it.
* Functionally, it ought to move and adjust as simply and naturally as possible. It should support a person in any position, at any task.
* Anthropometrically, it ought to do more than just accommodate large or small people; it should really fit them.
* Environmentally, it should use minimal natural resources, be durable and repairable, and be designed for disassembly and recycling.

At even the earliest stages, it became clear that the resulting chair was going to look radically different from all previous models. Stumpf recalls that he deliberately created a unique shape for the Aeron chair: "The human form has no straight lines, it is biomorphic. We designed the chair to be above all biomorphic, or curvilinear, as a metaphor of human form in the visual as well as the tactile sense. There is not one straight line to be found on an Aeron chair."

The reactions of focus groups were often that it looked odd, too technical, or faddish. But everyone who sat in the chair immediately discovered the comfort of the mesh fabric and the benefit from the high level of adjustability. The Aeron chair comes in three sizes: A, B, and C or small, medium, and large. Research field studies showed the relationship between the size of the person and their preference for chair size made having three chair sizes necessary. The reclining tension was designed to accommodate adjustments of individual preferences and weights of the user. The back can be stabi-

➡ **2003** Aeron chair with polished aluminum

PREVIOUS SPREAD
1994 Aeron chair

lized to provide continued support for intense keyboard use. The arms can adjust vertically and laterally to accommodate physical needs and work style preferences.

The pellicle material that forms the seat and back solved the problem of heat build-up and allowed for the free flow of air, moisture, and light. An office furnished with Aeron chairs feels more open and visible than offices with solid chairs. It created a new office aesthetic. Transparency, soon seen in such products as Apple's transparent iMac computer, became a design movement—to make technology less opaque, less intrusive, and to communicate the inner workings of things. The chair then becomes part of the person who uses it and the environment that surrounds it.

The Museum of Modern Art (MoMA) was so intrigued with the form, function, and aesthetics of the Aeron chair that they accessioned it into its permanent collection prior to the public introduction. Introduced in Europe in 1994, the Aeron chair became such an immediate success that Herman Miller manufacturing had to be reconfigured and expanded to accommodate the higher than expected sales. The chair quickly became the standard for the high-tech industry—and any company that wanted to be seen as current. The design and business communities' acceptance of the Aeron chair can be seen in its being recognized as "The Design of the Decade" for the 1990s by *Business Week Magazine* and The Industrial Designers Society of America.

← **2003** The Aeron chair with one of several alternative pellicle materials.

1994 Lumbar support Pellicle classic

2003 Posture fit Pellicle tuxedo with polished metal

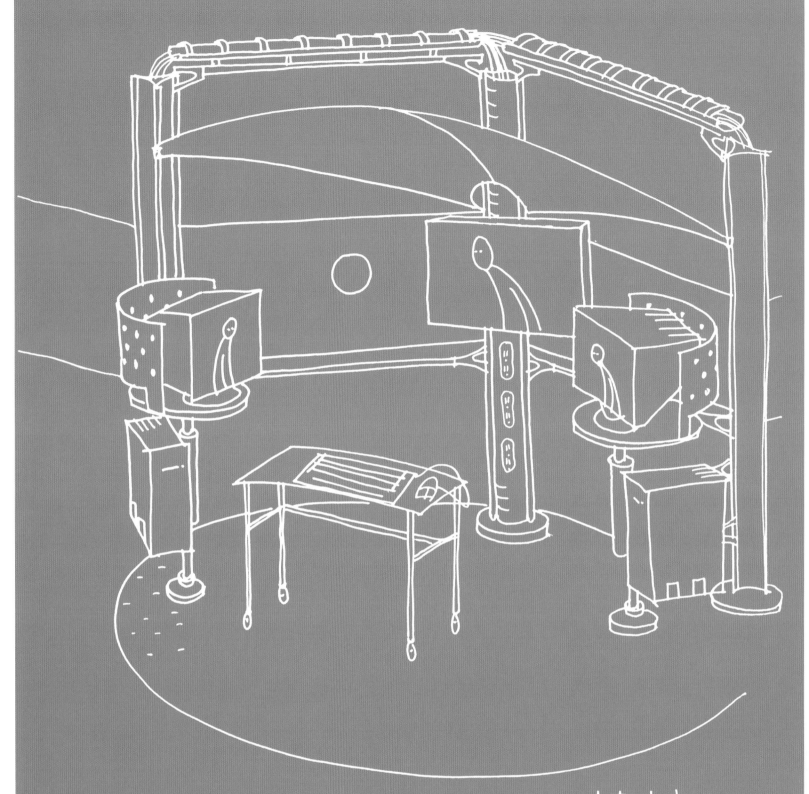

zigzag with pods, low distribution
and flat panel

birsel
3·22·98

CHAPTER 13 : **KNOWLEDGE WORK**

RESOLVE

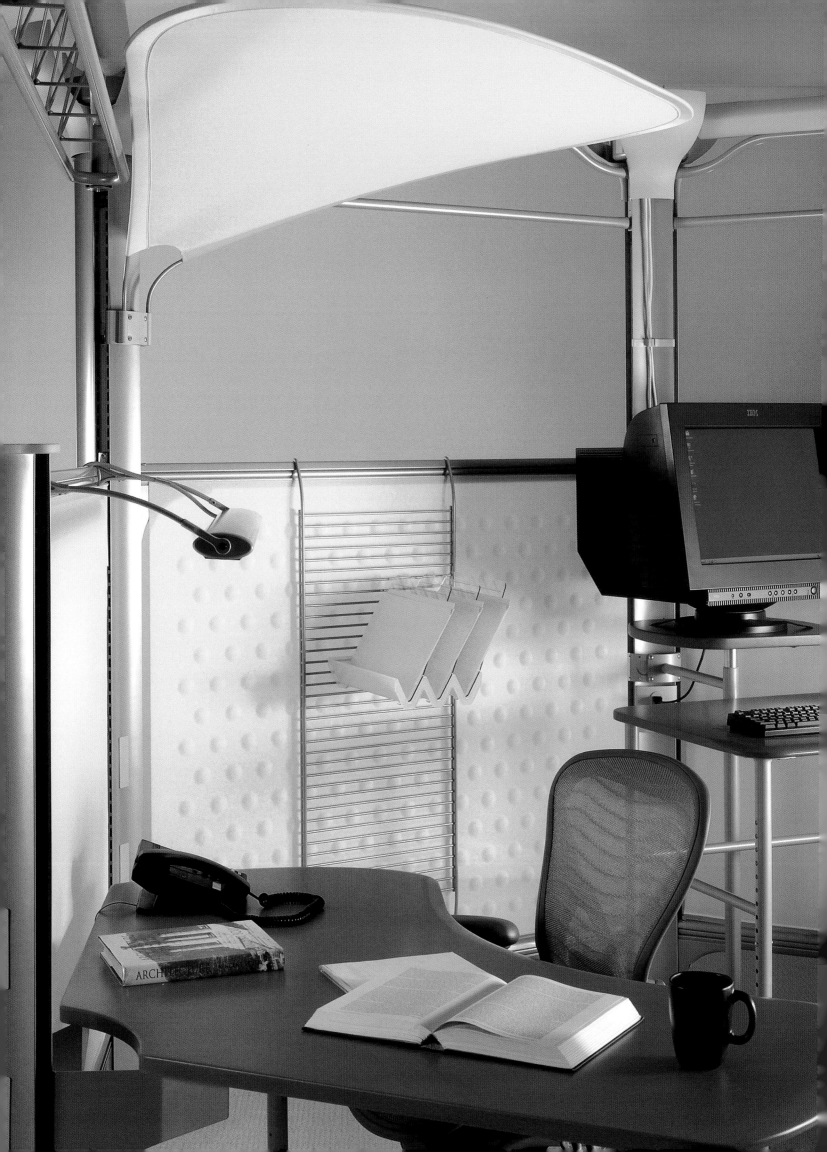

ACCOMMODATING NEW WORK STYLES

MORE THAN FORTY YEARS AFTER THE INTRODUCTION OF
ACTION OFFICE, THEY SOUGHT A RADICAL DEPARTURE.

↑ **2000** Ayse Birsel

← **2003** Individual workstation

PREVIOUS SPREAD, RIGHT

2000 Resolve zig zag application

The speed of office growth, change, and relocation dramatically increased in the 1990s with the economic boom and the rise of the Internet. Change, or churn, of physical offices grew more than 14 percent over the decade, and businesses needed an even more flexible office system that made disconnecting and reconnecting easier.

Herman Miller recognized these changes and collaborated with designer Ayse Birsel to reexamine the work environment and resolve (or *re*-solve) today's workplace issues. Birsel, who says, "I'm not very good at giving new form to old answers," welcomed the opportunity to dig behind the surface.

They quickly identified ways that offices were changing. Individual work spaces were becoming smaller. Technology was becoming more important. Project teams, in which individuals came together for a particular task and then were assigned to other teams, were more common and necessitated highly flexible office configurations while preserving personal space for each worker. In addition, many companies were interested in presenting a more stylish office, which included allowing more natural light into the office.

Herman Miller, which created the open-office panel system (see chapter 5) and spawned the facility management industry (chapter 8), now experimented with a system, based on new needs, with no panels at all. More than forty years after the introduction of Action Office, they sought a radical departure.

The result, Birsel's Resolve Office System, which was introduced in 1999, is a simple system with poles and screens. The side elements attach at 120-degree angles—the angle of honeycombs and bubbles, and nature's most economical way to create a stable structure. Privacy and sun-screening are provided by scrims, which can be printed with an unlimited range of imagery, color, graphics, and different degrees of transparency. Paper files are movable, and data wires routed overhead—making it easier to reconfigure the spaces.

The obtuse angles also break up the monotonous grids of cubicles and aisles that fill so many offices. They create offices that are more akin to villages—fulfilling Robert Propst's intentions for the original Action Office in 1964. Although it is much more open visually, it provides audial privacy with a new technology that masks speech and makes it easier to concentrate.

Its efficiency extends beyond the office itself. Because it has a fraction of the components of a traditional office system, its pieces take up one-third of the space when in storage.

Although heralded by the design community, Resolve has been slow to be accepted by businesses. The economy surely plays a part. It was introduced just as the dot-com industry—the sector that most readily embodied the changes that Resolve accommodates—went into decline. Even companies that might benefit from its functionality prefer, for the time being, a more sober aesthetic. However, as seen with the collections of Gilbert Rohde in the 1930s, Herman Miller is not afraid to be ahead of the pack when it knows personal habits are changing. In many ways, Resolve takes the company back to its roots.

↓ **2001** Delta constellations with Aeron chairs

→ Concept sketch and layout by Birsel

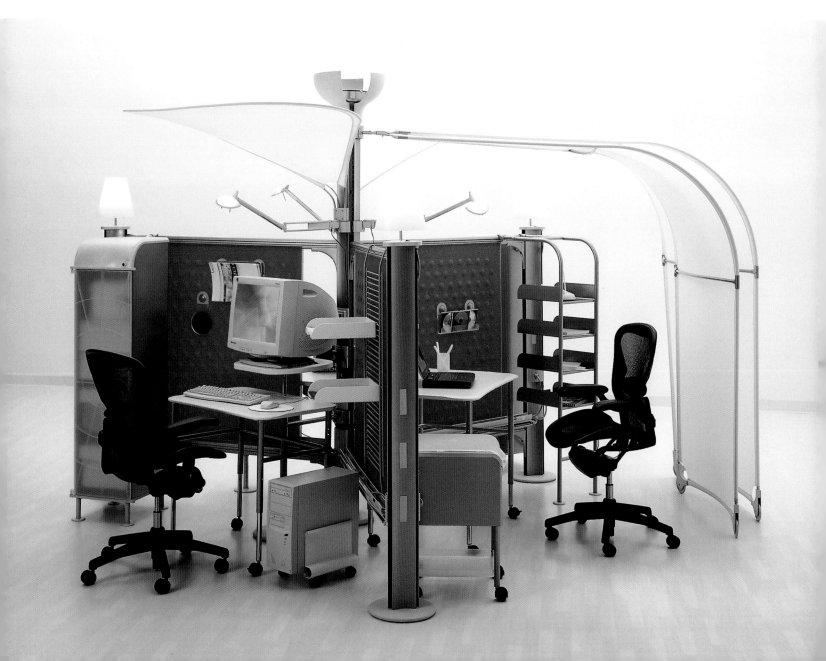

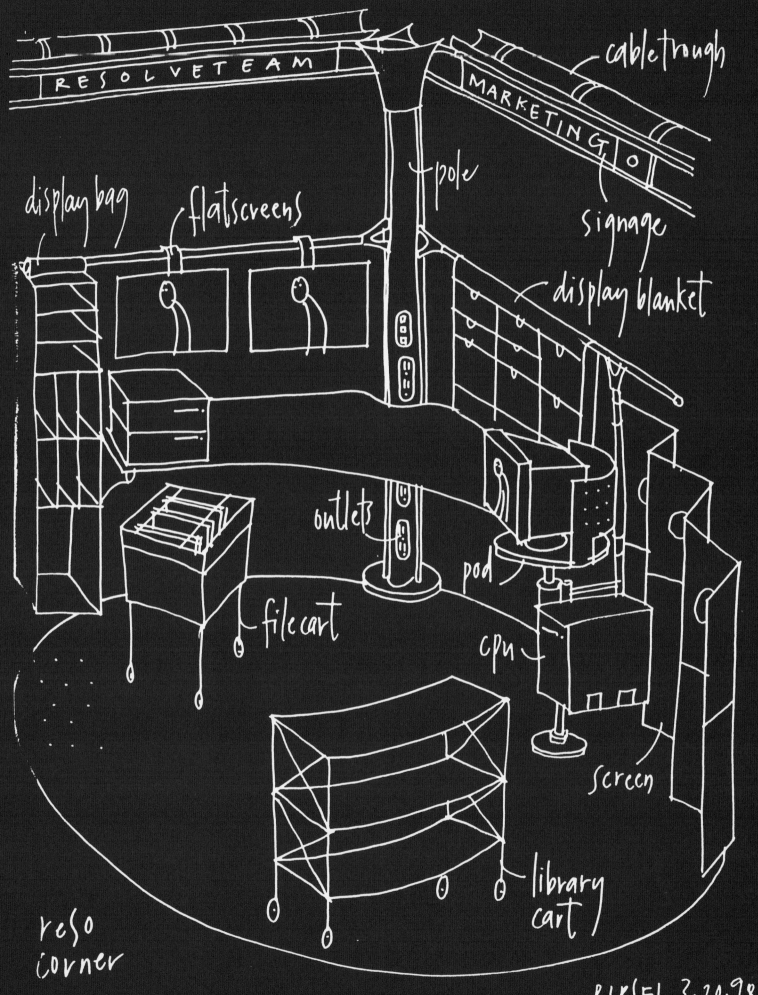

RESOLVETEAM

MARKETING O

cabletrough

display bag

flatscreens

pole

signage

display blanket

outlets

pod

filecart

cpu

screen

library cart

reso corner

BIRSEL 3.20.98

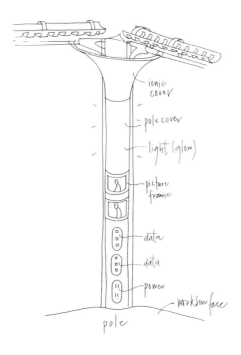

ionic
cover

pole cover

light (glow)

picture
frame

data

data

power

work surface

pole

Birsel concept sketches of
connection details for power
and data cable management

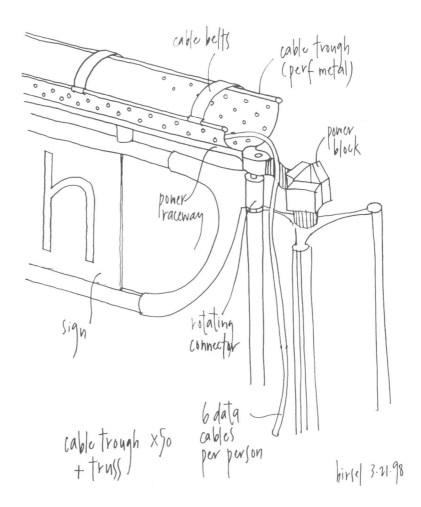

cable belts

cable trough
(perf metal)

power
block

power
raceway

sign

rotating
connector

cable trough x50
+ truss

6 data
cables
per person

birsel 3·21·98

← **2001** People technology connection

NAME	CONSTELLATION	W/ TABLES	AS FOLDING PAIRS	AS ZIG ZAG SPINES
HONEY ROOM				N/A
HALF HONEYS OBLIQUE				
HONEY PAIRS or HONEY HUB				
HONEY CLUSTER 6 HONEY PAC				
HONEY CHAIN 5				

NAME	CONSTELLATION	W/ TABLES	AS FOLDING PAIRS	AS ZIG ZAG SPINES
ZIG ZAG or (ZAG 2)				
ZAG 3				
ZAG 4				
ZAG 5				
ZAG 4 SPINE W/ DIVIDERS				

← Layout possibilites of Resolve with
120-degree connection

↑ **circa 2001** Resolve installation
with Aeron chairs

Corner Shelf

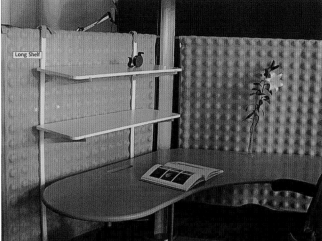

Long Shelf

Tall Shelf with
Side Covers

Tall Shelf with Display
Blanket Material

Three-dimensional models, prototypes of
Resolve, investigating materials, connections
and visual effect

↓ Resolve installation with 48-inch poles,
custom-screened graphics, and Mirra chairs

OVERLEAF

2002 Resolve demonstration
application with Aeron seating
and Eames aluminum group

CHAPTER 14 : **MIRRA**
STUDIO 7.5

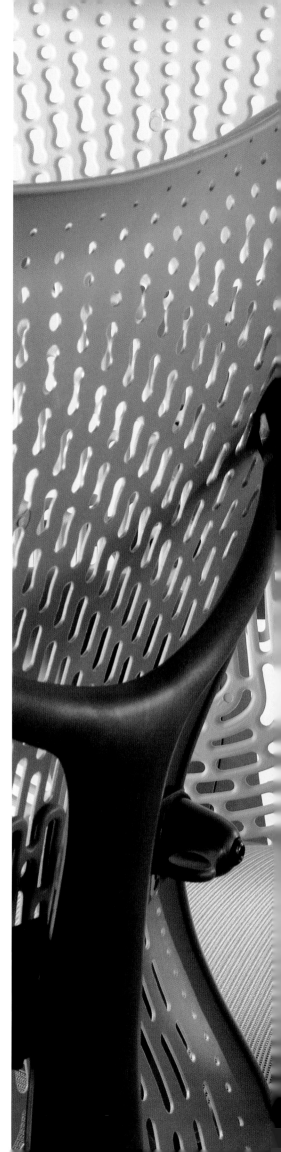

[RECOGNIZED NEED]

AN AFFORDABLE
ERGONOMIC TASK CHAIR

"THE CHAIR, AND THE COMPANY, CONFIRMS THAT GREAT
DESIGN AND ECOLOGICAL AND ECONOMIC SUCCESS ARE
POSSIBLE TODAY."

The increase of repetitive stress injuries in the workplace—and the increased amount of time white-collar workers spend in their office chairs—created the need for high-performance chairs at all price levels. Employers have come to understand the benefits of ergonomic seating, but often must meet restricted budgets.

A chair was needed that drew on the knowledge behind the Aeron but used new materials and manufacturing processes to keep the price low (the suggested price of the Aeron chair is around $850, while the new chair was targeted for a price of around $550). Studio 7.5 in Berlin was commissioned to work with an in-house Herman Miller team to develop the chair. In addition to creating ergonomic comfort at a better price, they were to meet environmental goals of high recyclability, high use of recycled content, ease of disassembly, and minimal parts.

Design inspiration came from nature, and Studio 7.5 hit upon metaphors that helped them envision what a chair could be: "From the geometry of a tree, to the smoothness of a curled leaf, to the flex of muscle fiber, to the changing colors of seasons and skies.... At first glance, nature's beauty seems the picture of simplicity. A closer look, however, reveals myriad intricate forces at work."

The collaborative design team created the Mirra chair, introduced in 2003. It provides both active and passive support for the user, a full range of back support, new uses for materials, and a new aesthetic. Bill McDonough, architect, designer, author, and leading force on sustainability, says, "Herman Miller's Mirra chair represents the most advanced and complete application of the Cradle-to-Cradle design protocols among any product manufactured to date. The chair, and the company, confirms that great design and ecological and economic success are possible today."

PREVIOUS SPREAD:

LEFT: **2003** Stacked Mirra backs in 8 colors

RIGHT: **2003** Mirra back detail

→ **2003** Mirra chair in several different colors

Studio 7.5, a German design firm, was composed of five designers—Claudia Plikat, Burkhard Schmitz, Nicolai Neubert, Carola Zwick, and Roland Zwick. The team has been involved for years in the design and development of products that improve the way people work.

They consider themselves "the grandchildren of the Eameses," and, like those pioneering designers, they are experts at observing how workers interact with their environments and finding ways to make that interaction more natural. Sharing a genuine passion for seating, they know seating as a science and work to bring it to another level.

Rather than relying on any individual in the firm, Studio 7.5 works as a team, without titles or hierarchy. The Mirra chair is a product of their collective imagination, talent, and persistence—along with a willingness to break the mold in order to create a chair that sets a new standard for comfort, fit, balanced ride, and visual refinement in its price range.

Studio 7.5 envisioned a chair that reacts to what people do. Part of the concept was to make the chair like a second skin, like a shadow of the sitter. From this concept, Mirra's passive adjustability was born. The TriFlex back, the AireWeave seat suspension, and the Harmonic tilt were designed to achieve a simple fit: Just sit on it, and it fits. There are only a few adjustment controls, and they are designed to be very intuitive.

Mirra was developed from common materials applied in original ways—such as the elastomeric seat suspension and molded polymer back that are used instead of foam and fabric. The relationship between materials and technology was pursued, similar in approach to the Eames work on mass-produced seating.

In fact, the material considerations for Mirra began with the end result in mind. Following the McDonough Braungart Design Chemistry Protocol—which defines the parameters on sustainability—Studio 7.5 considered the assembly and recyclability of the materials they selected. The result: A product that is 96% recyclable following the end of its useful life.

User testing, benchmarking, focus groups, tilt performance studies, and other methods were used to ensure the chair meets customer needs and provides advanced ergonomic performance. For example, research over the years has shown that the biggest concern users have is back support. In fact, back issues account for the second highest number of work illnesses. The designers took this to heart and focused on the back as an area of differentiation.

Herman Miller and Studio 7.5 also used results from the Civilian American and European Surface Anthropometry Resource (CAESAR) study, which surveyed body measurements of people aged 18–65, using the latest 3-D technology. Data from the study—the first full-body, 3-D surface anthropometry survey of the U.S. and Europe—helped ensure the chair fits people from the 5th percentile woman to the 95th percentile man. Simply put, they produced the perfect chair for everyone.

↑ **2002** Studio 7.5

→ **2003** Mirra with Resolve System

2003 Mirra chairs with upholstered backs

2003 Back view

This bouquet of forget-me-nots was used by Charles and Ray Eames to conclude their multimedia experience "Glimpses of America," produced for the 1959 American National Exhibition at the U.S.A.–U.S.S.R. exchange in Moscow. The film captured daily life in America through thousands of gathered images that were tape/synced to a score composed by Elmer Bernstein. Unable to come up with a way to end the seven-screen presentation, Ray went to her yard, picked the flowers, photographed them in her vase, and finished the show with that photograph on all seven screens. At its first showing, to the surprise of Charles and Ray, who were watching in the wings, there was silence when the film came to a close. They then saw tears in the eyes of the Soviet spectators, who for the first time had an understanding of life in America uncensored by Communist media. The Eameses did not know that in Russia, this flower is a symbol of friendship and loyalty. The impact on the audience was as an appeal to know America, an offering of friendship, and a shared understanding that we are all similar individuals.

It is my hope that the simple learnings from this book will be useful, not forgotten by businesses and designers, and will help to create a shared understanding of the value of design. Collaboratively, business and the design professions can make a most significant difference in our world.

THINGS TO LEARN FROM HERMAN MILLER

COLLABORATIVELY, BUSINESS AND THE DESIGN PROFESSIONS CAN MAKE A
MOST SIGNIFICANT DIFFERENCE IN OUR WORLD.

People and organizations learn by having a basis of comparison. Plato's "allegory of the cave" provides the recognition that without prior experience with a situation or an object, a person can't understand it. The design experiences of Herman Miller provide other companies the comparison for the value of including design as part of strategic planning.

The keys to Herman Miller's approach are the recognition and belief in the uniqueness of the individual. And while there wasn't one individual that could be said to be the single force, there is a common denominator that came from one man's experience.

Shortly after D.J. De Pree became the company's president, the plant's millwright died on the job. The millwright was essential to a furniture manufacturer. He ran the furnaces, which in turn fired the engines that turned the lathes that transformed wood into furniture. De Pree visited the widow to extend his condolences. She read some poetry aloud from a large book, and after several poems, De Pree remarked on the beauty of the work and asked about the poet. To his surprise, the woman's husband, the millwright, was the writer. De Pree began to wonder, "Was he a poet who was also a millwright, or a millwright who was also a poet?" Either way, he had not recognized the special gifts and talents of his employee, and he vowed to find ways to value what was unique in each individual.

This experience made De Pree open to the ideas of others, so that he was able to consider and accept Gilbert Rohde's views of a changing society, and to experiment with new designs to address that society. He was able to seek out and embrace George Nelson, a visionary, a novice in furniture design and a critic of the industry. He was able to support Nelson's belief that the role of design must be integral to the company.

In 1948 Nelson asserted that there was a market for good design. "This assumption," Nelson insisted, "has been more than confirmed, but it took a great deal of courage to make it and stick to it." And Herman Miller has now stuck to it for more than seventy-five years.

Design *is* good business. When De Pree took over the old Star Manufacturing in 1923, sales were $262,000. In 1930, when Rohde joined the company, the Depression had reduced sales to $76,000. By 1944, with a new way of selling and a solid commitment to modern design, sales were $450,000, and in 1968, following the peak creative period of Nelson and the Eameses, sales were a whopping $16 million. In 2000, they reached $2.2 billion.

Over these decades of growth, Herman Miller's focus on design and real needs never declined. In a 2002 *Harvard Business Review* article, Herman Miller CEO Mike Volkema stated, "One of the things I think I understand about Herman Miller is that innovation is in our DNA. We have this cultural personality and a reputation that attracts people who like new ideas."

This ongoing commitment to design and innovation has evolved into an organizational structure called the "Creative Office." Mike Volkema, now chairman, will spend more of his time with this strategic initiative. The purpose of the Creative Office is to provide a process for balancing new business models with new product development, coordination of the work of outside collaborators, and to harvest in a "more deliberate way" some of the great ideas that emerge. In the past, the company had hit upon ideas that were too far ahead of their time, but later proved to be huge successes. Through the Creative Office, new needs are recognized and new products and services continue to be generated. Significant new solutions to ever-changing needs in the built environment for the workplace and more are planned for introduction in the fall of 2004.

So what can be learned? What does Herman Miller's experience provide to other companies? Here are five suggestions.

1. Stay focused. The renowned business consultant and corporate strategist Peter Drucker has said, "The art of good management is the art of astute repetition." Design's important position at Herman Miller was established by De Pree and Rohde and has been supported ever since. A 1998 Herman Miller "Blueprint for Corporate Community" says, "Throughout our history, with the help from people like George Nelson, Charles and Ray Eames, and many others, we have met the challenge of change through design. We start with the real world, with real people, and with real problems. Design is about solving those real-world problems. . . . All of us can design solutions to improve our products, our services, and our businesses. Great design leads us to new insight, understanding and innovation. Through good design we serve our customers better than anyone else."

2. Ask questions. Common to all of Herman Miller's activities, from product design to architecture, graphics to organizational structure, are two questions. What are the needs being addressed? What are the constraints? Herman Miller designers help identify issues needing to be addressed. Bill Stumpf, for example, has posed the question, "What are the basic needs of today? Work has been rationalized to the point where all the joy has been removed. How do we enhance the joy of work? In spite of the discontinuity of places, how do we help the worker develop a 'sense of place'?"

3. Respect the differences in others. One sign of a healthy individual or company is the ability to have a relationship with others whose opinions differ from your own. D.J. De Pree was a deeply devout individual; George Nelson was an atheist. Their strong mutual regard strengthened both of them. Such self-comfort with knowing who one is as an individual or a company allows for openness to new ideas.

4. Collaborate. Herman Miller engages designers not as employees, but as consultants or experts outside the corporate structure. Outside designers provide a better view, are less encumbered by corporate politics or worry of employment, and generate an energy that breeds optimism. It is easier to make an exciting idea feasible than it is to make a feasible idea exciting. The most creative solutions derive from multiple disciplines working on a common problem.

5. Understand the problem before developing the solution. Sometimes a company gets excited about a product before it has determined what need it fills or what problem is being solved. A product introduced with fanfare about its style may receive recognition, but rarely becomes financially successful in the long run. Charles Eames once said, "Identifying the problem is the first 50 percent of finding the solution. Solving the problem is the last 50 percent—and 95 percent of the work."

All business is a holistic activity. Too often businesses are run as reductionist organizations, with decisions based on financial data without consideration of intuition and a holistic view. Design is relegated to a cosmetic function. Design is a holistic discipline, fed with data. It makes connections between seemingly disconnected elements and incorporates the intuitive process.

Recently, as part of leadership development, a cross-section of Herman Miller employees who are not designers worked on a new definition of design, in order to better recognize the field's role in the company's future. Starting with the understanding that creating a consistent culture of design is good business, they presented their definitions of design to senior management as the beginning of an ongoing dialogue. Two of their definitions follow:

* **Design is function with cultural content.**
    Objects and spaces reflect the times in which they are designed. They embody the social, technological, and cultural attributes of their moment.
* **Good design solves problems. It is honest, graceful, functional, and egalitarian.**
    Honest: It clearly communicates the essence of the problem. It exposes connections; materials are what they are. Nothing is hidden.
    Graceful: There is a fluidity that starts with the person first. It finds inspiration in nature; things that are organic.
    Functional: It solves a problem; it does what it is supposed to do.
    Egalitarian: It is for all people. It doesn't concern itself with status or entitlement.

The purpose of design is to solve problems. The relationship between design and business is synergistic. Herman Miller has long—and continues to—set an example of design as a fundamental part of strategic planning. In an interview with Peter Lawrence, chairman of the Corporate Design Foundation, published in the magazine @*Issue*, Tom Peters, business guru and author of *In Search of Excellence,* said, "The dumbest mistake is viewing design as something you do at the end of the process to 'tidy up' the mess, as opposed to understanding it's a 'day one' issue and part of everything."

Herman Miller makes no such mistake. There, design is part of everything. The company continually strives to grow its understanding and ability to improve the quality of our working and living environments. Now that's design.

ACKNOWLEDGMENTS

In addition to the encouragement from my wife Claudia, there are many people who have been most helpful in preparing this book. Specifically, the very capable folks at the Herman Miller archives: Gloria Jacobs, Linda Baron and Ernie Dykhuis. Additional helpful HMI friends include Mike Stuk, Steve Frykholm, Wayne Baxter, Diane Garone, Dave Peterson, Mark Schurman, and Ray Kennedy.

Thanks to Clark Malcolm, writer, friend, and the talent behind many a book.

Thanks for access to images and permission for their use from The Eames Office, particularly Bern Styburski. Thanks to Eames Demetrios, author, filmmaker, and brainstorming colleague.

Many thanks to my colleagues at the Greystone Group for allowing me the time for this new venture of writing a book.

Thanks to Lois Maassen for permission to adapt the Herman Miller timeline and the assistance of her team.

Thanks to my editor Elizabeth Johnson. I now understand why so many authors praise this key role in a book's development. Thanks to graphic designer Sara Stemen for her ideas and adaptability. And thanks to the publishing shepherd, Holly Rothman, for guidance and diligence through a new process for me.

Thanks to Steve Hamp, for his friendship and stewardship of America's history of innovation.

And particularly, thanks to Marg Mojzak of Herman Miller for the Home, without whose encouragement and support this book would not have happened.

PHOTO CREDITS

All images provided from the Herman Miller archives, except on pages xii, 82, 93, and 230, where the images are courtesy of the Eames office.

BOOK REFERENCES

Abercrombie, Stanley. *George Nelson: The Design of Modern Design* (MIT Press, 1995).

Demetrios, Eames. *An Eames Primer* (Universe Publishing, 2001).

De Pree, Hugh. "The People and Principles at Herman Miller." *Business as Unusual* (Herman Miller, 1986).

De Pree, Max. *Leadership Is an Art* (Dell Publishing, 1989).

Neuhart, John, Marilyn Neuhart, and Ray Eames. *Eames Design* (Abrams Press, 1989).

Webb, Michael. *George Nelson* (Chronicle Books, 2003).

INDEX